BOY PREACHER

A Supernatural Journey!

ALEJANDRO ARIAS

FIRST EDITION

ISBN: 978-1-939748-33-1

Library of Congress Control Number: 2013952781

Published by
NewBookPublishing.com, a division of Reliance Media, Inc.
515 Cooper Commerce Drive, #140, Apopka, FL 32703
NewBookPublishing.com

Printed in the United States of America

Disclaimer: The views and opinions expressed in this book are solely those of the authors and other contributors. These views and opinions do not necessarily represent those of New Book Publishing and Reliance Media Inc.

Contents

Contents, Continued

Endorsements

Alejandro Arias is a young man touched by heaven for extraordinary purposes in his generation. "Boy Preacher- A Supernatural Journey," is a remarkable story of the miraculous transforming power of God and how the anointing of the Holy Spirit can radically use a person, even as a child. Alejandro's story is an inspiring account of a young man and his journey as the "Boy Preacher." You'll love this book!

— *Pastor Gary Costello,*
Awesome Church, Sydney, Australia.

Alejandro's life and ministry bear testimony to the unmistakable call of God on his life.

You will be blessed as you read about his miraculous calling and the miracles that follow his ministry. I highly recommend this book, as it will stimulate and build your faith in our Heavenly Father.

— *Pastor Patrick Humberstone,*
Oceans and Cornerstone Church, Perth, Australia.

This unique book is the inspiring biography of a young child who dramatically encountered the call of God through a heavenly visitation. You will be challenged by the passion of this young boy preacher, known as "The Little Pastor", and his insatiable longing to know the Holy Spirit and to serve God with a pure heart.

From small beginnings, conducting services to children in his street, today he travels the world with a powerful revival anointing and a contagious passion to see the Gospel preached and souls won to Jesus. Through this book you will encounter personal revival as you are drawn into the heart of God and His passion for the redemption of all mankind.

— *Pastor Alan Wills,*
Bridgeman COC, Brisbane, Australia.

"Boy Preacher- A Supernatural Journey," is a story of ageless appeal, a testimony that has the power to change your whole outlook in life. Alejandro Arias is a passionate and anointed evangelist, and, as he shares with you the work of the Holy Spirit in his own life, you too will learn how to develop a childlike, loving relationship with Him.

— *Dr. Javier Espinoza,*
Chairman of Christian Fellowship, Latin America.

Alejandro Arias is undoubtedly a man chosen by God. From an early age he was set apart to become a key vessel in the expansion of the Gospel of Jesus Christ. For that reason, I am sure this book will be for you a genuine testimony of the greatness of God, and of what He has in store for all who recognize Him as Lord and Savior.

— Dr. Alberto M. Delgado
President of the Hispanic Ministers
Association of Greater Miami
Senior Pastor, Alpha & Omega Church.

Acknowledgements

The writing of this book would not have been possible without the help of the great men and women, family members and church leaders who have helped me throughout the years on this amazing journey.

I would first like to thank my dear wife, Rebekah, for her massive contribution of time, insight and advice. Without your love and unending support, I would not be where I am today. I am so thankful that we can serve our Lord together. Thank you for helping me make this dream come true.

I would also like to thank my parents for their love and for the many sacrifices they made for me to pursue the calling of God on my life. Thank you, most of all for your commitment, dedication and faithfulness to God.

I also would like to express my gratitude to my dear friend and spiritual father, Orlando Lopez Varela, and his wife, Xiomara de Varela, for your support in coaching me while I was just a child and for investing your time, love and resources in me.

I am also indebted to my Pastors, Wilbert and Sonia, for their cooperation and their input in my life. Thanks to my mentor and friend, Pastor William Magaña for helping me learn the ropes. I also want to thank Pastor Alberto Delgado for helping us with Alejandro Arias International Ministries' transition from Costa Rica to the USA. A special thank you to my beautiful Aunt Maria Pervatt for her tireless work with AAIM throughout the years. Thank you to Kathy and Glenn Shepherd and Marcos and Dana Gunter, who became like second families to me while I was living in the States.

I am so thankful for the wonderful AAIM Board of Directors that God has given me in the USA and Australia. Thank you all for your vital advice, your valuable wisdom, and most of all, your friendship. I would also like to thank my dear friend and colleague, Evangelist Eton Mills, for taking the time to revise and edit this manuscript. I also express my gratitude to the team at New Book Publishing for helping put this book together and for all their input into this project.

Above all, I would like to thank my best friend, the Holy Spirit, for His inspiration, counsel, support and His strength throughout the years. I thank Jesus, for saving me and for calling me into His service and I thank my Heavenly Father, for His eternal love!

Foreword

It is rare to meet a young man with such passion and unreserved commitment as Alejandro Arias. Born in Costa Rica, he started preaching the Gospel from a very young age – when most children would be playing games with their friends. Not this little boy! One must understand that the call of God is not limited by age but directed solely by divine appointment. Such has been seen in the life of young Samuel, in an age where God's call came to a young man with an ear to hear.

I first met Alejandro two years ago when he and his Australian wife, Rebekah, moved to Victoria, Australia.

As a Pastor in the south west of Melbourne and Regional leader in the Australian Christian Churches network, I hit it off with Alejandro during our first meeting. There is a spiritual resonance that happens when two Kingdom-hearted people walk into the same room. As time has progressed, we have built a strong connection.

What stands out most to me is that Alejandro is the real

deal. He doesn't just talk faith – he walks faith. God has opened up amazing doors of opportunity throughout this nation and the nations. Alejandro is true to the call and gifting on his life to preach the Gospel wherever he goes. In a supernatural way, God moves with Holy Spirit power; particularly through his preaching and the laying on of hands.

I trust you are inspired and blessed by his book.

Pastor Mal Macleod
South West Christian Church
Melbourne, Australia.

Chapter 1

Alejandro, You're In Heaven

Rays of light streamed through the window, gently heating my room as the sun rose higher in Alajuela, Costa Rica. It was going to be a beautiful, warm day in the valley, the perfect kind of day for a public holiday. That morning, I enjoyed a refreshing sleep-in past 6 a.m., the time I would usually have to get up for school. Although La Pradera Elementary School was only a few blocks away, we would rise at this early hour to get ready, have breakfast, and still have time for devotions with my faithful praying mother, Damaris.

The lie-in that morning also enabled me to catch up on some much-needed sleep. Being fairly studious, I was something of a "night-owl" and would often stay up until late, trying to memorize the answers for the long tests. When I had finally gotten up and done my chores, I began to contemplate what I could do with the rest of my day. Remembering that I had not yet met with my best friend, Jesus, I suddenly felt a strong compulsion to lock myself in my room and pray.

I went to my room, turned on my CD player, and began to worship. I had become accustomed to doing this and to waiting upon the Lord for as long as it took for His presence to saturate my room. Sometimes it would be only ten minutes into my prayer time before He was there, other days I had to persevere and press on, waiting for Him to come. That morning, the presence of the Holy Spirit was instantly there, so overwhelmingly that I actually felt I was breathing in His anointing.

Immersed in worship and studying His Word, it must have been at least three hours before I realized that I had completely lost all awareness of time. I had ended up lying on the floor with my face down. Sensing that some thing particularly supernatural was about to happen, I looked up and suddenly my eyes were opened to a celestial realm: I saw a tall, glorious being standing a few meters away from me. As I gazed at him in wonder I felt a strange sensation, as though I was leaving my body. When I looked down I saw myself lying on the floor, wearing a white tunic with a gold sash around my waist.

A great peace descended on me and instinctively I knew what I was to do. Without hesitation I drew near to the angel and followed him. The angel turned and walked through my bedroom wall and I found that I was able to do the same. My spiritual body was able to pass through the solid and the material, just as Jesus did when He appeared to His disciples after the resurrection.

On the other side of the wall, I found myself standing in the middle of the living room, where my brother was watching TV. I could hear my mom preparing lunch for us in the kitchen. I seemed to view all of this in third person however, without any of my family members being aware of my presence. The angel and I walked out onto the terrace of our two-story house, which opened out into expansive views of our neighborhood below. The angel took me by the hand and suddenly it was as though we took off, traveling through the sky at a cosmic speed I have no words to describe.

As we passed through the atmosphere and into outer space, I caught a glimpse of planet earth far below. Our solar system flashed by, and in the blink of an eye we were in a completely different place. I found myself walking through a large corridor, which eventually opened out and led to a large wall. The massive wall appeared to be made out of seamless, gleaming white marble and was so beautiful it was unlike anything I had ever seen on earth. We walked around the wall for a few minutes before I realized that it encompassed a city. I marveled, thinking how amazing it was that even before there were any walled cities on earth, walls existed in heaven. Their purpose, however, seemed not to keep enemies out, but to reflect the greatness and glory of our God, who describes Himself as a wall of fire around His people and His city:

> "'For I, says the Lord, 'will be a wall of fire all around [Jerusalem], and I will be the glory in her midst.'" Zechariah 2:5 (NKJV)

Before long, we came to one of three doors in the wall. I paused, gazing up in awe at the huge, solid wood structure, which was something like a gate you might expect to see in an old English castle. Seeing that the door was sealed, I waited for the angel to open it. It was then that he spoke to me for the first time, not in the kind of audible, physical voice we hear on Earth; but rather it was as though his spirit was speaking to mine. He spoke without words, and I *felt* rather than heard what he said.

"Alejandro, you're in heaven."

Suddenly, a mighty, rushing wind blew past and blasted the door open. Thick, blindingly bright mist spilled out of the doorway, and when it cleared, I could see a long rectangular room with a table stretching to the other end. The table was beautifully made up, set with fine, white linen and adorned with red satin runners. There were also golden serving bowls filled with many different kinds of fruits. Each place was set with the finest gold and silver cutlery I had ever seen. Everything was in a state of completeness and utter perfection.

The elegant vista continued even as I looked upward; the sheer scale of the room was utterly unfathomable. The walls were made of gold and were covered with elegant wallpaper to halfway up. The ceiling was covered with engraved blocks of solid gold and set with intricate diamond patterns. Ornate lamps hung from the ceiling, casting their bright glow over the entire room. When I looked closely, I realized that they did not seem to run on electricity or flame, but drew their power from some other energy source. They were lit by the presence, the very glow of the glory of God – just as is described in the Scriptures:

> "The city had no need of the sun or of the moon to
> shine in it, for the glory of God illuminated it. The
> Lamb is its light." Revelation 21:23 (NKJV)

How wonderful it is that in heaven all light is a reflection of God Himself! Because God is the Light, there is no need for any kind of energy or power resource. He sustains everything by His very being!

> "This is the message which we have heard from Him and declare to you, that God is light and in Him is no darkness at all." 1 John 1:5 (NKJV)

I turned my attention back to the table – a table so long I could not see the end of it. There was a sense that all the i's had been dotted and all the t's crossed in preparation for a big event. Everything sat ready, in silent expectation. The angel took me by the hand and in a flash we were transported to the other end of the table.

"Alejandro, this is the place where the Marriage Supper of the Lamb will take place," the angel said. He then turned and pointed to a large, ornate wooden chair, which looked like a throne, placed at the head of the table. "And this is where the Bridegroom will sit on that glorious day."

I was still trying to take all this in when we were translated in the Spirit again to the city wall. Walking along the wall, near where we had first come in, we came to a second door. This door was colonial-style with a large silver handle. Once again, I felt the blast of wind rush past me, blowing the door open. The angel led me inside by the hand and I was met with a sight so glorious I could hardly comprehend it. We were standing in a colossal amphitheater, filled with thousands of angels on their feet, worshipping God in perfect unison. In choral harmony they sang – a symphony of voices beyond human comprehension, their lyrics most beautifully profound. Some played musical instruments while some sang – all arranged in sections and all synchronized to perfection.

Although they worked in teams, it was also clear that the angels each had their own particular ministry. Some conducted music, while others danced, waving colorful flags and banners. I was amazed to see that in heaven angels worship God in similar ways to us, using many of the same instruments and symbols.

The most noticeable thing about the angels was their sheer delight. None worshipped half-heartedly. No one simply performed. They radiated pure joy as they honored and gave praise to God Most High, the Creator and King of the Universe. As I watched them, I felt completely overwhelmed by my desire to join them; the best choir I had ever heard. With all the compulsion of a child, I let go of the angel's hand and began to run to the front of the auditorium.

An angel stopped me and politely asked, "Your name, please?"

He then went over to a large open book and began to leaf through its pages. With a broad smile, he looked up and pointed the way forward, saying, "You may come." How my heart leapt when I heard those words! As I carefully made my way up a flight of stairs at the front, I could see that the steps were embedded with sapphire and emerald. At the tops of the steps was a huge platform covered in gold. A river flowed from the center of the platform, the platform's backdrop was a living window; a panorama of green meadows, rivers and a spectacular rainbow. Hovering over the platform was a bright cloud, churning with lightning and rumblings of thunder. Although invisible to me, I knew somehow in my spirit that deep within that impenetrable cloud was the very throne of God. As I passed by the cloud, another throne came into view – one at the right hand of the Father, full of light and majesty. Seated upon the throne was the most beautiful person I had ever seen, one whom I recognized instantly: The Lamb of God, The Great Triumphant One. I felt the glory of God wrap around me, enveloping me. The next thing I knew, I was sitting on His lap – the lap of Jesus Christ. I saw the marks in His hands and feet. Overwhelmed with love, I wrapped my arms around Him, never wanting to let Him go!

Time ceased to exist while I was with Him. I was so thrilled and content I could have stayed there with Him for the rest of my life. Jesus pointed in front of us and I saw something like a large screen opening up. By this time, the angels had ceased playing and everything had gone silent. On the screen, I could see myself, but looking much older. I was standing in front of a great mass of people of various nationalities and preaching to them with great fire and boldness.

As long as I live, I will never forget Jesus' words to me as we viewed the vision, "This shall be your ministry on earth."

With that, the screen shut down and vanished. As I turned around to face Jesus once more, I heard a voice call out, telling me, "It's time to go!"

It was my guiding angel at the entrance of the auditorium, beckoning me. Oh how I wanted to hug Jesus and never let go! In spite of clinging to Him tightly however, I suddenly found myself back outside the city walls, walking side by side with my angelic tour guide. The final room I was taken to was like a great library. Its walls were paneled in oak, and gold furniture was scattered about on luxurious rugs. There were books, piled up in categories according to their color. Angels sat behind large rectangular tables, looking almost like school pupils as they wrote in and stamped books. In a constant flurry of activity, they were opening books, closing them and putting them back on the shelves.

The curious thing was that all the while they also looked downward, at the floor! When I looked, I saw why. Beneath the floor was something like a crystal river with images floating in it. The river seemed to serve as a high tech screen in which everything on earth was recorded and transmitted to heaven! It was impressive to see the angels "downloading" new information and data from the screen and recording it in their books every time a new soul came to Jesus! Just as I was beginning to take in the whole scene, the angel took me by the hand and suddenly we were descending, heading back to Earth!

I remember opening my eyes and wondering how many hours had gone by. Strangely, one of the first things I recall was my stomach rumbling. Lunch was long gone, but the experience I had would stay with me always. I kept the vision locked tight in my heart and did not speak of it to anyone, until many years later. "This is the story of the calling I saw in the vision coming to pass, and of what He has taught me along the way…"

Preaching in the park,
Alajuela, 1999.

An altar boy at La Pradera
Catholic Church, age 5.

Family. From left to right: Myself, my cousin Karen,
my sister Karina and my brother Francisco.

*My parents,
José and
Damaris on their
wedding day.*

First crusades in Gautemala, age 12.

Evangelistic camp meetings in Colombia, age 13.

Outreach crusade in San Felipe, Venezuela, age 14.

*Beginnings in the United States, preaching at
Cornerstone Church in Davie, FL, age 16.*

Chapter 2

God Is Love

On August 10, 1985; my parents were married at the local Catholic Church in La Guacima, Costa Rica. My mother, Damaris Naranjo Arroyo, was only eighteen-years-old and my dad, almost thirty. He had a grocery store at the time and was doing relatively well. My dad had been a small business entrepreneur since the age of twelve, but he wasn't succeeding as much as he could have owing to one problem – much of the money he earned was wasted on his dear old friend – the Bottle. Because of his strong addiction to alcohol, Dad didn't always get home early. He would go to the bar and drink until he was so drunk his friends had to carry him home.

My mom used to tell us a funny story about their honeymoon, which typifies dad's behavior when he was under the influence of alcohol. They were staying in a farmhouse they had rented for the occasion and had gone to a "turno" (a Costa Rican term for a party) that night. During the course of the evening, he upset mom and she decided to leave the party early.

Later that night, as my dad was stumbling back to the cottage in the dark, he heard a faint noise…a growling sound. Unbeknown to him, by taking a different route he had alerted the farm watchdog – a strapping German shepherd. When the dog began barking and pursuing him, my dad had no choice but to run for his life. When he finally made it to the cottage, he discovered that the door was locked tightly and bolted. In desperation, he pulled out some of the glass louvers in the window, climbed up, and managed to get half of his body inside. With the German shepherd unable to get to him, he leaned on the table on the other side of the window and fell asleep in a state of drunken exhaustion.

While that particular incident was funny, it signified the beginning of a tumultuous and often painful marriage, especially for my mom. From that day she began to carry the cross of being married to an alcoholic, with little sign of hope or change in my dad. On May 16, 1986, my sister Karina Maria was born at Mexico Hospital in San José at about 8:16 a.m., a glimmer of hope and a bundle of joy, for she was the first child.

On November 1, 1987, my mom was ready to give birth to her second child. Most of our relatives thought it was going to be a girl but my mom had a deep conviction it was going to be a boy. My sister was just under two years of age when I came into this world. Some of my uncles and aunts suggested naming me "Armando." My mom didn't like that name however. Instead, she named me "José Alejandro;" José being to honor my father and grandfather, who have the same first name. In Costa Rica it is traditional for a boy to carry the first name of his predecessors to honor the family name. It is an old tradition, although not followed in all cases.

Mom says that I was a chubby baby and quite healthy when I was born. I had to be put in an incubator two months later however, due to a very bad case of pneumonia. That was one of the many hospital stays I would experience in the future, and I remained a sickly child for a long time.

On October 30, 1988, a year and two days after my birth, my youngest brother came into the world. He was something of a surprise, since my parents had not been planning to have any more children. My mom thought she'd taken ill, but when the pregnancy tests came back positive it was a big shock for everyone. So there we were – the Three Musketeers. When we went out as youngsters it was the two boys squeezed into the stroller and my older sister walking alongside.

La Guacima, where we lived at the time, is about 15 km from Alajuela, the main city. Sometimes, depending on the traffic and how slow the bus went, it would take up to forty minutes to get there. Going to the city was quite an expedition, and you can imagine three children crying and demanding equal attention! Alajuela is the second largest city in Costa Rica, and it is where the international airport is located. We used to go on family trips to the airport. For us children it was like a fun park with the great view of the planes landing and taking off. We used to sit there and sip on a Granizado- a Costa Rican smoothie, watching those big jumbos taking off. I had a great fascination with those aircraft; one which I would later realize was God preparing me for much travel later in life.

One day we went to visit our grandparents, Abuela Mari and Abuelo Fran who lived very close to us in the small town of Las Vueltas. Very much an introvert when it came to interacting with other kids, I took delight instead in conversations with adults, even at the age of three. I remember that day after lunch chatting away with my grandparents when suddenly; out of nowhere, a dove came into the house and flew over us. As my grandma recalls, I lifted my hands and said without even thinking about it, "The Holy Spirit is upon me!" Grandma, a faithful Catholic with no deep relationship to Jesus Christ, let alone the Holy Spirit, gave me a funny look and burst out laughing!

When I was five, I would celebrate Saturday Mass. Not at a church though mind you, but a private Mass at home! I would wake up early in the morning, put on my "priestly vestments" (which was really just Dad's over-sized shirt), and run up and down the streets, giving out invitations to the children in the neighborhood and calling for them to come. Although some laughed at my antics, to me Mass in the garage was a very serious affair. I would prepare a table and neatly spread a nice tablecloth on it. And, when I was sure everything was ready, I would ask my father for some white cookies to represent the bread and my mother for grape juice to represent the wine. Once the children had gathered, I preached a brief sermon.

Although some listened, others were only interested in playing. As it was all very serious business for me, I became cross and called them to attention. After twenty minutes of chattering away about the story of creation and about God's love, I prayed for them and had them make the line to receive communion, trying to imitate what I had seen done during Mass at the church. Some of the children made the line two or even three times, until I realized they had only come for the free snacks!

Although I was only five and did not know how to read, when I preached to the children, bible verses and bible stories would spring to mind. All these things surprised my father, who wondered, "Where is Alejandro getting these words and ideas?" He was not a regular attendee, either at my little Mass or at the Catholic Church, preferring instead to work hard all weekend and to go to the fiestas in the evenings. On such occasions, he and mom would get us to sleep early with a special warm drink, made with lettuce.

Sometimes we were taken along too, but I never really had the heart to participate in the festivities. In direct contrast to my siblings, who went to the dance floor to play and dance with the rest of the children, I preferred to stay seated and watch until the end of the evening. It was very difficult for my parents to understand why I was so different, and they were often puzzled by my behavior.

My father asked me many times, "Alejandro, why don't you go and join in and dance with the other children?" "I don't feel right being here, daddy, and I don't think God likes these parties." I answered him.

I did not realize it at the time, but even from a very young age the Lord Jesus had been guarding my heart, causing me to pull away from my father's lifestyle. Having an entrepreneurial bent, my dad had opened several bars in the city and eventually ended up owning more than six liquor stores, as well as two pre-established bars. My father was also well known in the community as a party organizer and would occasionally close off the streets to bring in music groups and large discos. He appeared to have it made, but in reality, his life was in complete bondage to the vice of alcohol.

Many nights, my father didn't come home until early in the morning. Things had reached the stage where drinking became his main priority and everything else came second. Sometimes, he wouldn't even open the businesses for days. Everything came to a head when our finances finally failed. I remember saying to him one night, "Daddy, God has a plan for you and He can change you." In those times when there was so much strife and desperation in our family, I persistently urged him to change, but ultimately change was a long way off. Alcoholism is a stronghold and it takes a long time to confront it. Eventually I could do no more than just look on and pray in my heart, asking Jesus to transform our family. There were times when I overheard fights between my parents in the early morning. During one such argument, my mother finally told my father that she wanted a divorce. He agreed, but on one condition - that she move far away, so he would never have to see her with another man. The following night, they called a family meeting and asked us the hardest question we would ever have to answer, "Who do you want to live with, mom or dad?"

Although at school my hand always shot up during question time, this night I stayed silent, waiting for my siblings to respond. My sister Karina, who had seen my mother's tears and suffering, replied, "I am going with mommy." My brother

Francisco replied the same with a giggle, being too young to understand and perhaps thinking it was all a game

As a six-year-old, I did not fully comprehend the enormity of what was happening to our family, either. But when it came my turn to speak, I believe the Lord gave me the right words, "I'm going with both." My parents did not rejoice at this statement, but even so, I had the firm conviction that Jesus already had plans for our family. God has been faithful to fulfill those plans for us, and today we are able to look back and marvel at what He has done and continues to do in our lives.

The divorce plans proceeded and the lawyer who was in charge of my mom's case began to accelerate the process. To compound matters, this man had fallen in love with my mother and was trying to flatter her with pretty words. The guy was doing everything possible to succeed in his love mission, but what he didn't realize was the best lover in the world, Jesus Christ, was about to captivate her heart!

The weekend rolled around and it was time for the big parties again. This Friday, my father had already gone to the bar early and would not be coming back until later that night. Unbeknown to me however, today would be different. God had a wonderful surprise in store that none of us could have imagined.

My mother turned on the radio that afternoon as she usually did, to listen to her favorite music program. Not enjoying secular music, I turned to go outside and play with my friends. As I did so, I could hear her scanning through the channels for her station. She recalls how suddenly she felt as though someone had stopped her hand on the dial. A Christian broadcast filtered through the speakers, and the three most beautiful words she had ever heard invaded our living room, "God is love."

"But who loves me," she thought, "If my father abandoned me when I was little, and my husband is divorcing me?" Immediately, the Holy Spirit began to work in her heart, revealing the depth of God's unconditional love for her. Kneeling down in the living room, tears streaming down her face, my mother gave her life to Christ. Never had I seen her cry the way she did that day, and it really made an impression on me. After she had gotten up and written down the address of the church broadcasting the message, she got ready and went to San José to attend one of the services.

Today, my mom speaks of this experience with great joy. It was truly supernatural and glorious. I saw the change in her and was amazed. I was very grateful for all that God was doing in my family. But I knew that something had really fundamentally shifted when my mother undertook to pray for my father. Gradually peace began to reign in our home. Their arguments eventually ceased and life changed completely.

Around that time, we moved to La Pradera, a town about 10 minutes away from La Guacima. My mother started attending the Church of God in town. I was seven when she first invited me to go along with her, although I had not yet accepted Christ. It so happened that ten days after my mother's conversion, an announcement was made at the Sunday service that an open-air evangelistic campaign would be held in our neighborhood and that there would be a guest preacher. I was very excited and I began to count down the days! When the time arrived, the meeting was held in one of the neighbors' backyards. Close to two hundred people packed the place and the atmosphere was quite beautiful. The presence of God filled that place and the evening became an unforgettable night for me. Many people came to Christ and there were amazing miracles. By the second night, I had made up my mind and planned everything carefully in advance. Knowing there would be a surge of people towards the front after the altar call, I made sure to sit closer to the platform. When that glorious moment came and the preacher gave the invitation to accept Christ, I literally leapt off my seat and sprinted to the front, determined to be the first one to get there.

The pastor seemed overjoyed as he contemplated the dozens of people who had run to the feet of Christ. He continued to invite people to come forward and began to pray for us. There, in God's presence, I felt as though a current of electricity were passing through my body. Tears rolled down my cheeks. Having waited such a long time to know Him and to see His glory, my heart pounded with joy and excitement. The service ended all too soon and I wished the campaign did not have to finish. The following morning when I got up, the first thing I said to my mother was, "I don't want to be a priest any more, I want to be a pastor." With a smile, she replied, "Yes, you will do it." What she did not know was that God had already been preparing me for a ministerial calling.

Chapter 3

Hearing His Voice

I looked at the clock and saw that it was 7:30 a.m. By now, my parents would already be out attending to their business. Being the weekend, I decided to go and help my father in the shop. Later in the day, however, I began to feel unwell and tired, so I decided to ask my father for the house keys and head back home to rest. Upon entering the house, I was enveloped by the refreshing coolness of the living room. I turned on the television, sat down, and was beginning to get comfortable when suddenly I heard a voice call my name. I wondered who this could be, since I had already said goodbye to my parents at the shop and had been sure I was alone in the house. Clutching the keys tightly, I looked in the direction of my mother's room, where the voice seemed to come from. In that instant, I saw something that made my hair stand on end – a pure, white light, shining brightly out of the doorway.

I stood gazing at it, transfixed by the supernatural sight. I felt all fear melt away and a sense of reverence and awe surround me. The same audible voice called me for the second time, and an intense, tangible feeling of peace flowed through my arms, legs and entire body. I was speechless. When I was called for a third time however, I could no longer bear it. I ran from the house and went looking for my parents.

The question will always remain in my mind, "What would have happened had I recognized the voice and stayed?" It would be years later before I realized that I had experienced the manifest presence of God and heard the voice of Jesus for the first time. He was calling me into His service.

I enjoyed school and liked that it was only a five-minute walk from our house. My favorite subjects were Social Studies and Geography – anything to do with planet earth and its history and culture really. The Principal of La Pradera Elementary School, Lucyna Zawalisnki, was on a teaching exchange from Poland. She was a strict lady, but also very nice, and during recess I would often visit her office to ask her questions about her country. Sometimes, when we left class, I would stay back so I could walk with her to the bus stop. I would continue talking with her, fascinated with the stories she told.

One day, I asked my father to get me a map of the world so I could pin it up in my room. He bought me a large one, and I would spread it out on the floor, lay my hands on the various countries and pray for revival to break out in those places. I would pray passionately for lost souls and ask the Lord Jesus for the nations. What I didn't know at the time however, was that one day God would give me the privilege of preaching the Gospel all over the world...

My parents owned a grocery store and a bar at the time.

My brother Francisco and I were in charge of putting the stock on the shelves and keeping the aisles clean and tidy. We had so much fun and we loved helping our dad after school. I was in charge of the inventory from time to time, and when we needed to buy more merchandise I would accompany Dad on his business trips. During the evening, the shop was not such a pleasant place to be in though, as it operated as a bar. The ambience wasn't exactly friendly, so I used to detest going there for anything. It was in the bar, however, that I first saw the need of men for a greater hope and I believe it was there that my evangelistic ministry really started.

As my passion for preaching the Gospel of Jesus Christ increased, my visits to the bar to pass out tracts became more frequent too. I felt inspired to write Christian messages on napkins and pass them to clients. My dad did not like my evangelistic strategies, however, and continually admonished me to cease all such activities. One day, he was so upset that he told me off in front of clients and said that he never wanted to see me in the bar passing out tracts again. I can't honestly say I paid much attention. One way or another, I never passed up the chance to witness to people, even preaching to my dad occasionally.

Following my conversion, the desire to know Jesus intimately grew more intense each day. The calling He had planted in my heart really began to take root. I did not know at first exactly how to personally draw near to God, but I made up my mind to find out. I began to accompany my mother whenever she visited the small church down the road from our house, and I was hungry to attend meetings whenever possible. The congregation would meet out on the patio and some of the most glorious services I ever attended happened at that humble little church. If for some reason my mother was unable to attend, I would grab the New Testament I received at the evangelistic campaign and make a getaway! For days and nights, I would dedicate myself to learning more about the word of God. In this way, I grew spiritually and The Bible became my most cherished book.

I listened to Christian radio and kept myself informed of the Christian events happening in Costa Rica. The various "Marches for Christ," for example, which I would ask my parents to go to. They also took me to prayer vigils. Around this time, my father had a job as a window installer. One day I asked him, "Daddy, could I have a special placard made of glass, for the National Christian March? Will you build me one?" He smiled and said, "Yes, I will make you one." I was ecstatic. When the day came for the "Rally for Jesus," my father had my glass placard ready. It was so heavy though that my mother had to help me carry it! We all went walking through the streets of San José, praying for our city and our nation. The march finished with a praise and worship concert with different delegations from around Costa Rica represented and my own pastor preaching the Word.

Nearby, there were dozens of Christians handing out tracts to passersby. When I saw this, I became very excited – passing out tracts was my favorite hobby. I was always going around my neighborhood passing them out in the street. If someone wouldn't open the door to me, I simply slid the tract underneath!

I approached one of the men on the evangelistic team and asked with a shy smile, "Sir, can I help you give out the tracts?" The man looked surprised and said, "Of course you can help me, boy." He handed me a wad of tracts. Feeling as though Christmas had come, I took off to distribute them with much joy. My mother, who by this time had lost sight of me, was growing increasingly worried, wondering where I was. I had gotten myself deep into the crowd and was positively lost! After her frantic attempts to locate me were unsuccessful, she recruited some of the ushers to join the search party. Half an hour later, I was still obliviously handing out tracts when I heard an announcement over the loud speakers. Something about a lost child, whose description sounded…remarkably like me! Reluctantly I made my way back to the platform, where my mother met me with a sigh of relief. We then headed home. Even on the bus back though, I could not resist handing out some more tracts.

Passion, the Ingredient of Success!

One of the things that I learned when God first called me, was that passion is the thermometer of our destiny. It will cause us to do what we do with excellence and with zeal. If you are passionate about football for example, you will talk about football. You will know all there is to know about it. You will know all the players' names. You will love the game! If you are passionate about computers, you will know about the latest software and the capabilities of each program. Or, if you are passionate about acting, you will study your lines diligently and ensure that you attend each rehearsal.

The reality is that passion is the driving force of life. This must especially be the case in our relationship with the Lord. Indeed, we are instructed to:

> "Love the LORD your God with all your heart
> and with all your soul and with all your strength."
> Deuteronomy 6:5 (NIV)

If we do this, we will be given a completely new outlook on life. Our dreams, goals and entire life's purpose will be transformed.

Chapter 4

Prayer Vigils, Drama Plays And The Bus Stop

Prayer is the vital secret of the Christian life and, as believers, we must have a prayer life, making prayer a daily habit and enjoying it to the fullest! Prayer vigils were my favorite type of event to attend, and I remember having such a great sense of expectation leading up to them. They took place in various churches and provinces of Costa Rica. When a vigil was held in another province and a commute was necessary, sometimes the church hired a bus to take people along to the meetings. Taking the bus also promised the additional fun of stopping somewhere to eat along the way and sometimes staying up all night for the long trip home!

Those services were amazing. Pastor William Magaña was one of the conveners of these prayer rallies. When he took the microphone and prayed, the whole place was shook by the presence of God! The dance time during praise and worship was my favorite! All the kids would go up front and dance with a joy and excitement so contagious that many adults joined us too!

As my hunger for prayer began to develop, so did my desire to serve God in the local church. From passing the offering plate to singing a song, doing a mime with the arts department and going out on street evangelism missions in the neighborhoods, it was all so much fun. Sometimes we would perform in other churches, or we would be invited to perform with other groups. This was all preparation for the days to come. As a child, I was very aware that God was doing something in my life and that one day, it was all going to come through.

I took an interest in the arts, particularly in drama. I often played the role of a prophet. On other occasions I was an angel. But never the devil or any of the demons! I carefully declined such offers when they came my way. (Thank God that our teachers never obliged us to play such a role!) Marisol and her husband, Wilbur, worked as a team teaching the children in our church. I am forever grateful to this couple for teaching me to love God and serve Him with excellence and diligence. I remember Marisol as a very disciplined lady who never missed an opportunity to teach us godly principles, even in rehearsals. Our plays became so well known that we earned a few awards in the local region and were even invited to perform at secular school graduations.

The Bus Stop

It was 3 p.m. and everyone in our class eagerly awaited the wail of the last bell Scarcely had it sounded before we were out the door, running, chatting with friends and rejoicing that another school day was over.

I went to the bus stop where I thought my older sister would be waiting to take me home, but was alarmed instead when she did not show up. She must have forgotten and gone on ahead. I would have to wait for the next bus. Becoming more anxious by the minute, I learned that the next bus would not be due for at least another hour. Rather than wait that long, I considered walking home. The school I was attending at the time was too far away though, so I decided to stay put. Little did I know however, that God had a special purpose for my being there at the bus stop!

A lady wearing a sad, world-weary expression came and sat next to me. I had a sudden impulse to speak to her about Christ, so I asked her if something was wrong. Appearing surprised that I'd asked, she told me about some of the situations she was facing. The moment came when I had the opportunity to evangelize, so I began to speak to her of Jesus and shared how He had rescued my family. I wasted no time in praying with her for salvation and, before I knew it, the bus arrived! With a brand-new smile, she thanked me and handed me some money to buy candy. I now know that God put me there just for her. That would be just one of the many occasions in which I found myself witnessing to strangers in different places and under a variety of circumstances.

Although naturally a quiet and reserved child, I was a chatterbox when it came to talking about Jesus and His salvation plan. Every time I jumped on the bus and had an opportunity to talk to someone, I would do it without hesitation. It was all so much fun!

Riding the bus one day, I noticed an oddly dressed young fellow sitting next to me. I said, "Hello," but his reaction was not exactly warm and friendly. Undeterred, I asked him what his religious background was and, to my amazement, he said he had none. In Costa Rica it is a rarity to come across an atheist, but when you do, it is a golden opportunity. Time to talk about Jesus, again! He went on to explain why he did not believe in any God. When I heard his statement of unbelief, I got myself into position like a hunter ready to pounce. I looked at him and refuted his arguments with such a conviction that only the Holy Spirit could give! After the long conversation, he finally gave up and said he was going to think about it. As he was about to get off the bus, I shook his hand and said, "Jesus loves you." He smiled somewhat wryly and left quickly, but at least he had something to think about. As I look back now, I see that the ministry God was giving me was starting to take shape, even at the bus stop.

Chapter 5

What Is Impossible With Men

It was another day at school. I was sitting at my desk listening to the teacher, when suddenly I felt a sharp stabbing pain in my abdomen. The pain grew stronger and stronger until it washed over me in intense waves. Eventually it became so bad that I had to alert my teacher, who called my father to pick me up. This was a routine exercise during my childhood, as there had been many times when my father had to take me from school directly to the hospital, usually due to asthma attacks.

After a brief check-up at the hospital, I was sent home. The pain began to ease and soon I was able to fall asleep. But when I awoke, it kicked back in, stronger than ever, so my mother decided to call an ambulance. Hours of examinations and X-rays at the local hospital revealed that I had appendicitis and would need an operation.

It was 3 a.m. by this time and the surgeon was off-duty, so I was transferred to the National Children's Hospital in San José.

Once there, the doctors began to repeat the examinations I had already undergone in the hospital in Alajuela. Finally, at 7 p.m., I went into the operating room the operation was successful, but strangely, I was not released the following day, as was the standard procedure. Instead, I was subjected to yet another series of exams. This happened every day for five days, until finally, on the sixth day, my mother decided enough was enough. As the chief medical officer stepped into the elevator, my mother grabbed his hand, imploring him with tears in her eyes to tell her what was happening. He gazed at her for a moment with a look of compassion before answering, "Ma'am, your son has a problem with his right lung. We have discovered a massive tumor that covers part of that lung and part of his heart, and we are trying to see if it is operable. But I don't know if there are many options."

Returning to my bedside, my mother knelt down and sobbed. Although I did not understand why she was crying, I said to her, "Mommy, what is impossible with men is possible with God." Even after she explained to me exactly what was happening, somehow my conviction did not fade. Having been planted like an anchor in my soul, my faith rose up within me and proved firm. Nonetheless, when they finally allowed me to leave the hospital, my mother and I headed home with heavy hearts. We had not yet broken the news to anyone else in our family and there they were, waiting outside the house for us, happy and ready to celebrate the "success" of the operation with a small welcome-home party. We could not bring ourselves to spoil it for them and so we let the festivities continue. My pensiveness that evening was belied by a deep sadness.

I remember my mother sitting on the couch every night after that, weeping and crying out to God. I also got on my knees to pray, putting my hand over my lung and declaring that I was healed. It would be 6 months before the doctor re-examined me. But God gave us favor and my mother had the opportunity to speak of my case to the Director of Cardiology at the National Children's Hospital, who said, "Come tomorrow, and I will see if I can help, and we can conduct some more examinations."

That night, there was a healing service at the nearby church we regularly attended. When I heard that they were going to pray for the sick, I went to my mother and asked her, "Are we going to the service tonight? They are praying for the sick!" With a weary look she said to me, "No, Alejandro go and rest, you can't go because of your lungs." Disappointed, I went to my room and knelt down to pray. I began to pray that God would touch my mother's heart so I could go. She'd been so discouraged by my illness that she hadn't attended church for weeks. Yet, I could sense in my heart that something good was going to happen this night. So I returned to her and asked again, "Mom will you take me to the meeting?" "Okay." she said reluctantly, "Let's go. But I will have to keep you warm." She wrapped me up in a thick blanket and we walked to the church.

I felt the sweet presence of the Lord Jesus as soon as we stepped inside the building, and suddenly my mother began to cry. We had arrived very late and the pastor was in the process of closing the service. Suddenly, he stopped what he was doing, pointed to me, and said, "Thus says the Lord, the miracle that I will do in your life, shall be a testimony to the nations." I began to weep with my mother. We felt as though a mantle of fire had enveloped us. When the service finished, we went straight home, ready to get up very early the next day and take the bus to the hospital. At about 4 a.m., I heard noise coming from my mother's room. Realizing that she was in fervent prayer for me, I went to her and said, "Trust in God that He has already healed me."

That morning, the doctors X-rayed my lungs and heart. While we waited for the results I walked up and down the corridors in intense prayer, confessing my miracle. The medical staff passing by me looked on with surprise. I imagine they were wondering what I was doing!

After three hours of waiting, the doctor came out of his office and looked seriously at my mother. Pausing for a moment, he said, "Ma'am, I can't explain what has happened in your son's case. All I can say is…God is good." The instant I heard those words, my heart filled with joy. The doctor invited us into his office to see the x-ray results. Pointing to the first one, he said, "As you can see, here is where the tumor was." He then pointed to the second x-ray, "This is a miracle! I can't explain it, but as you can see, the tumor has disappeared. Not only did it disappear, but there is also a scar on the lung, like that from an operation." While the doctor recovered from his shock, I stood there praising God, in complete awe of what I had just seen! The first thing we did was find a public phone and call everyone in my family to tell them that Jesus had healed me. After months and months of waiting and hoping, God had honored their prayers and performed a miracle.

Sometimes we find ourselves in moments when we are cut down and threatened by different situations in life, occasions when our faith is challenged and tested as gold is refined by the fire. Those are the times when we need to meditate upon the God of Israel and His indescribable exploits. In such situations, when we have to take His inheritance and make it ours. When the enemy targets us, we should never bend ourselves for one instant to the evil one's designs and threats. Let's keep in mind that our God is righteous and that He will always give us the victory.

Remember, dear friends that Christ has triumphed over death. He took all our sins and sicknesses on the cross of Calvary more than 2,000 years ago, annulling every act of evil and making us free through His death and resurrection.

> "...He was pierced for our transgressions, He was crushed for our iniquities; the punishment that brought us peace was on Him, and by His wounds we are healed." Isaiah 53:5 (NIV)

When I meditate upon this scripture, that He took all our sicknesses and we have been healed, I take into account that this is an absolute truth that was established in the past and can be taken hold of by all the generations after. All we must do therefore is confess and believe in these truths that are valid for all eternity. Numerous times, the Bible tells us of the great stories of men and women who made history with their immovable faith. Let us also then, by activating our faith, shake the earth and move the heavens.

Chapter 6

Lord, If You Will Heal Me...

I remember praying and making this vow to the Lord, "If you will heal me, I will serve you for the rest of my life." Not long after my healing, those words took on real significance as we began to have family services at home. Every Wednesday evening, we had family prayer time. Sometimes, the neighbors were also invited. On one special occasion, my grandparents (who lived about two hours away) were present with us on the Wednesday. That particular day became very special indeed. In the morning after breakfast, my mom said to me, "Alejandro, tonight it is your turn to preach." I was not expecting to preach, thinking that she or my grandmother would. Usually the children's roles would be: my brother on the "drums," clashing some pots and pans, my sister singing and leading worship, and me taking up the offering. But to preach the main sermon – wow! I was so excited I could hardly contain myself!

I chose from my two favorite themes – the Coming of Christ and divorce, (two topics I often "preached" to my parents about) and began to work on my sermon. In spite of all my efforts, however, my siblings still fell asleep on the couch halfway through my sermon. (Okay, so maybe a feature-length film was shorter than my overzealous first sermon!) But little did I know, God had something special that he was going to do later that evening.

When we began to pray to wrap up the meeting, a different kind of atmosphere pervaded the room.

One of the things I had most desired and prayed a long time for was that when I lay hands on people, they would receive the power of the Holy Spirit. I didn't want to just pray. I wanted to be used by God. The thing that really ignited this passion was watching the program, "This is Your Day," with Pastor Benny Hinn. I was inspired as I watched thousands of souls coming to the feet of Christ and being filled with the Holy Spirit. I was always keen to watch the preachers praying for the people and seeing what happened through the laying on of hands. Although by that stage I already had the opportunity to pray for friends, family and neighbors on various occasions, I had never actually seen the power of God manifest. Yes, I prayed and people were happy, but I was not satisfied. My greatest desire was to see the manifestation of the power of the Holy Spirit.

That night, when I placed my hands on my grandmother and began to pray for her, I felt as though a lightning bolt fell from heaven into the center of our circle. Minutes later, I realized that I was on the floor beside my grandmother, crying and speaking in tongues! When I did stand up, I found that everyone was under the same anointing. My grandmother stood up and gave me a huge hug, saying to me, "Dear grandson, God is going to do great things with you." These words went deeply into my heart, and from that day, my quest for deep friendship with the Holy Spirit intensified.

It was this insatiable longing to know the person of the Holy Spirit and to preach the Gospel of Jesus that made me do things that many considered a little out of touch with reality. Because I was something of a dreamer with a vivid imagination, there was the sense at times that no one fully understood me. I did everything possible, however, to ensure that no one would steal the dream from me of someday becoming a preacher. The following incident stands out in my mind, illustrating just how that dream sometimes confounded the adults in my life.

A Note Home

The school bell rang and my classmates bolted outside. To my surprise, however, my teacher requested that I stay behind for a moment. Without divulging why, she wrote a note and stuck it in my schoolbook. I was too afraid to read it, so I stuffed my books in my bag and set out for home. The walk seemed to take forever that afternoon. All I could think about was the note. Why had my teacher written the note? What was it about? Had I misbehaved? Would I be in trouble? All these thoughts swirled around in my mind like confetti in a snow globe. I was puzzled. I had never received a note before. Occasionally, there were newsletters and such things, but these were given to everyone in the class. Why was I the only one who received a note?

I arrived home in silence that day, dumping my bag in my room and making no mention of the dreaded note. Despite my best efforts, when my mom asked for my backpack to see what homework I had, she discovered the note in the front of my book. She spent a few seconds reading it before calling me over and asking, "Why does your teacher want a meeting with us, Alejandro? What did you do?" My stomach in a knot, I could only respond faintly, "I don't know."

Straight away, my mom got ready and went over to the school to meet with my teacher. The following morning, Mom said I did not have to prepare for school. This was going to be a day off and we were going to visit someone. Because we routinely went for medical appointments, I thought that perhaps we were going to see a doctor. But Mom took me to see a man I had never met before and left me there with him in a room full of books. He was very friendly and asked me many questions – especially about my faith in Christ. Although I did not understand his sudden apparent interest in such things, I delighted in the opportunity presented me and began to evangelize the man.

He continued to question me on a range of other topics and then gave me a piece of candy, telling me that I had done very well and that I could go.

I reunited with my mom, who was waiting outside and the man re-appeared, saying simply, "Ma'am, your son does not need help. Perhaps his family could use it instead."

It was only later that I discovered I had been taken to a psychologist.

When I was a little older, I came to realize that my behavior as a child was not typical and sometimes alarmed my teachers or parents. It was strange for my teachers, for example, to see me setting up my pencils in front of me at my desk and pretending to preach to them. My parents would also hear me each afternoon playing alone, preaching to my toys, which were set in rows for a "church service." Sometimes, when I was feeling particularly creative, I would assemble my Lego blocks into a radio station and preach to the whole world. On the odd occasion, I would stand in front of the mirror and do a television program. Sometimes I would even enlist my brother Francisco to help "film" a thirty-minute segment, with the aid of a Coca-Cola bottle!

We started a Christian Children's Club, and I began preaching to other children on Saturdays. These meetings became well attended, and before long we were seeing kids being saved and taught the Word of God. These children were hungry to learn more about God and each week we had newcomers attend. What I did not fully realize was that everything I did was a training school for the days to come.

Chapter 7

Diego, The Bully

"El Padrecito! El Pastorcito!" To some I was "The Little Priest," to others "The Little Pastor." From time to time I would also hear the more offensive, "Abuelito," or "Little Grandpa!" These were some of the names that the kids at La Pradera Elementary School came up with for me. They were intended as insults, but knowing and understanding that to be a disciple of Christ I had to be willing to suffer persecution, I didn't take much notice of them. In time, some of my classmates began to approach me with questions about the Bible. I would then sit and have discussions with them, asking the Holy Spirit to help me answer their queries. In this way, little by little, God helped me to win territory, even in my own school.

Every school has its bully. My school was no exception. At La Pradera it was the infamous, "Diego." Being the tallest and strongest student in the school, we all had a healthy respect for him. Diego used to strike his fist against his palm in a threatening signal we all knew well. Someone was going to be ground to a pulp – preferably me! Because I somehow managed to escape Diego each time he tried to pick a fight (probably because my scrawny legs could outrun his barrel-like ones), he'd developed an insatiable thirst to hunt me down. I have never come across a child with such a near-pathological hatred. Diego seemed to want to get even with the whole world. I understood he was this way because he had grown up in an extremely dysfunctional, broken home.

Bearing this in mind, one day I decided to pluck up the courage to speak to Diego. When I began to address him, however, he refused to turn around or even look at me. Sensing that his anger was growing and his blood was beginning to boil, I took a couple of steps back, but in a flash Diego spun around, grabbed me by my shirt collar and lifted me up, pinning me against the blackboard. I had never seen him so enraged; it was like looking into the very face of a demon. Some of my friends saw what was happening and slipped away to call the teacher, but, before she could come, one of Diego's friends found out and advised him to put me down. When the teacher arrived, it was too late. She'd missed the incident and refused to believe my story.

It was my turn to help tidy up the classroom after school, but what I wasn't expecting was that Diego would be lying in wait for me when I left. There he was, standing at the school's entry and exit gate, blocking off the only means of escape. I began to tremble, until I heard a voice deep within me say, "This afternoon, I am going to show you my glory." When Diego began to taunt me and his friends started laughing, I felt as though I was surrounded by a pack of ravenous wolves wanting to eat me alive. Somehow though, I felt the Holy Spirit give me the strength to turn and face them. As Diego began to tire of making verbal threats alone, he walked menacingly towards me. Grabbing me by the shirt collar (a favorite maneuver of his), he shoved me against the ground and lifted up his fist, preparing to unleash the first blow on me. Suddenly, out of nowhere, I felt Diego wrenched clean off me. It just so happened that day that one of the teachers was leaving school later than usual and came across the whole scene. Just in the nick of time he turned up to rescue me from Diego's hands. The very next day, Diego was expelled from the school and the teacher who had not believed my story was dismissed!

I learned from this experience that God honors those who honor Him and He always gives us the victory as long as we trust in Him and stand on His Word. As the Scriptures say, we are blessed when we are persecuted:

"Blessed are those who are persecuted because of righteousness, for theirs is the Kingdom of heaven." Matthew 5:10 (NIV)

Many times, we feel intimidated when our comfort zone is threatened. What we must realize, however, is that to be persecuted should be one of the hallmarks of the Christian life. As His Word reminds us, we *will* suffer persecution for the love of His name:

"Blessed are you when people insult you, persecute you and falsely say all kinds of evil against you

because of me. Rejoice and be glad, because great is your reward in heaven, for in the same way they persecuted the prophets who were before you."
Matthew 5:10-12 (NIV)

Chapter 8

Give Me An Hour Of Your Time

Throughout my journey, there have been experiences God has given me, which I now recognize as being part of His blueprint for my life. There are events – some small, some big – in which I can see His divine fingerprint, even from when I was very young. It is my prayer that as you read this book, you too will be encouraged to believe God for the dreams He has placed inside your own heart, and run the race of faith to which you have been called.

On occasion, when preachers visited my church, it was not uncommon for them to prophesy over me. I remember one such incident from when I was eight-years-old. My mother tells me that the preacher that night lifted me up at the front of the church and stood me on the pulpit's handrail, prophesying that the miracle God had done in me would be a testimony to all the nations of the world. Once the service had finished, she adds, the preacher approached me and said, "I had a vision while I was preaching. I saw you preaching to thousands and it was in a country other than Costa Rica." He then prayed for me and gave me a big hug. Thus my passion to serve the Lord grew stronger every day.

One Hour of Your Time

Walking up the road from school one day, suddenly I heard a sweet, soft voice telling me, "Alejandro, give me one hour of your time after you return home from school, and I will give you the nations." In my heart of hearts, I thought, "But Lord, how can I give you one hour of my time, if I have to do my homework?" It wasn't really about the homework though. It was about having to give up my favorite 4 p.m. television show! "Cebollitas," was a popular teen comedy at the time and often proved even more attractive than lunch for my siblings and me. Many times we had to reheat our food because we'd been too caught up with the latest episode.

We all enjoyed watching the show so much and I didn't understand why God would be asking me for such a "big" sacrifice. Besides, I never really watched any other television programs or movies. And I was only 11-years-old! I had to ask myself what I wanted more – to watch television or to experience a closer walk with God. In the end, I chose the latter.

My Baptism in the Holy Spirit

My greatest desire was to be baptized with the Holy Spirit. One afternoon, after I had been asking God this for a while, I suddenly felt as though there was a strong wind blowing through my room and I began to speak in tongues. It was such a beautiful experience; the extraordinary thing was that all my windows were shut! My father arrived home and as he entered the house he heard someone speaking in another language. He became frightened, even more so when he recognized my voice. "What on earth has happened to Alejandro?" he thought. Meanwhile, in my room, I had come under such a powerful anointing that I felt as though the power of God had struck me like a lightning bolt. I went from being on my knees to falling face down on the tiles. When he heard the sound of the impact, my dad says it crossed his mind to call 911. Praise God that a few moments later I got up off the floor and began to pray again in Spanish!

This remains one of my most memorable encounters with God. I will never forget that special day when He perfumed my room with His dazzling glory for the very first time!

Chapter 9

Alejandro, I Have A Surprise For You!

O ne week my mom ran an outreach, showing Christian movies. The small event was to be held in an unoccupied building, which used to be one of my father's bars. The building was not being used since there had been an accident a couple of weeks earlier. It had been crashed into by a bus, which had rolled downhill, the driver appearing to have forgotten to put his handbrake on. Praise be to God that the bus was only parked a few meters away from the building and wasn't able to gather much momentum before it crashed! It was still enough to destroy the front part of the business though, but thankfully no one was killed or injured in the accident. Now I see it as being planned by God, who would use the incident to begin a work in my father's life.

My mother happened to be at home on the morning of the crash when we all went out to see what had happened. After assessing the situation, we thanked God that no one had been sitting on the sidewalk or waiting for a bus. It still gave us a great fright though; I recall my mother crying in my father's arms in shock. The only thing that comforted her were the words God had spoken to her that morning, "Daughter, God will cause all things to work for the good of His children." That is exactly what happened; a week after the insurance company repaired the building, it was used for evangelism and many presentations of the Jesus movie. To everyone's surprise, my father (who rarely attended church) went to one of the presentations. It was then that we knew God had begun a good work in his life.

Once the movie had finished and we were sitting around sipping hot chocolate, my father asked, "Where did you get these movies?" My mother replied that she found them in a Christian bookstore in downtown Alajuela and that he was welcome to come with her and have a look. To her utter amazement, my father got ready the following morning and went with her. While she was returning the movies, he stood staring at a pack of Gospel tracts on the shelf. Eventually the manager (who also happened to be the shop owner) approached him, asking if he needed any assistance. When my father asked how much the tracts were the manager suddenly became interested and asked what he was going to do with them.

This man, Orlando Lopez, also happened to be a missionary. When my father began to tell him about how I handed out tracts in the community, Orlando gave him a wad of tracts free of charge, telling him, "I would very much like to meet your son. Perhaps he can come with us to the central park on Saturdays and help us give out tracts."

As I was sitting on the sofa watching the news that afternoon, my father entered with a smile, saying "Alejandro, I have a surprise for you!" I immediately got up and went over to the table to sit with him. "Would you like to go this Saturday to hand out tracts in the park?" he asked. I happily agreed to do so, and with a big hug, my father gave me the tracts and the little letter of encouragement the missionary had written to me.

That whole week, I prayed and sought God with a great sense of expectation about what He was going to do. The days dragged by and Saturday finally came. I got ready early that morning and waited excitedly for the bus that would take me to Alajuela City. My father accompanied me that morning, something very special that would come to mark the beginning of our journey working together as a team, even in many different nations later on.

Revival in the Park

When I arrived at nine thirty, half an hour before the park service commenced, Orlando looked at me squarely and said, "Are you ready to preach?" This took me by complete surprise; by that time I had only preached occasionally to my family and to my neighbors, when they had invited me to share a message in their prayer group. I instantly said "Yes," but privately wondered what on earth I was going to speak about.

Around a hundred people were gathered in our corner of Alajuela Central Park, where loudspeakers were set up to carry the redemption message. When it was my turn to speak and

Orlando called me to the front, I remember feeling very small standing beside him. Indeed, my nickname around that time was "Tiny Big-Mouth."

When I opened the Bible, I felt for a moment as though I had forgotten everything I had studied. My knees began to knock together, but it certainly wasn't under the anointing! A few minutes into the message, however, I felt the familiar presence of my dear friend, helping me and teaching me what to say. Suddenly a powerful anointing enveloped me and all my nervousness evaporated. I felt the power of God fill the atmosphere in the park and as a result, seven souls came to the feet of Jesus that day. As I continued to preach in Alajuela Central Park each Saturday for about a month and a half, many souls came to Christ. Such was power of God in that place that some meetings there were around three hundred people present. Glory to God!

What had been a public park became a revival zone, where God healed the sick and freed the captives! There were some times when it was so full that passersby thought the crowds were there to see a circus act, which usually performed each Saturday. Confused, many came and joined the multitude, only to receive the greatest gift that any human being could receive, eternal salvation.

Chapter 10

Venezuela: My First Missionary Trip

It was the end of another long Saturday. The meeting had been very successful, with more than twenty people giving their lives to Christ. I was overjoyed, but at the same time a sense of sadness tugged at my heart. This meeting was the last in our six-week campaign. Tomorrow, my friend Orlando would be flying to Venezuela and life would return to normal for me. Little did I know, however, God had already been drawing up the next stage of his plans for me, even as I lay sleeping the previous night. He had visited Orlando as he prayed in his room and instructed him to take me with him to Venezuela. A new chapter was about to begin.

That afternoon when I went to say goodbye and give him a hug, Orlando asked me the one question I never imagined he would ask: "Would you like to come with me to Venezuela?" Feeling like my heart was going to jump right out of my chest, I revealed that was precisely what I had been praying for but never imagined in a million years would actually happen! My sadness instantly became joy and the discouragement, excitement; all I could think of was going up in a big airplane, something I had always dreamt of! For years, I had watched the airplanes land and take off at the airport, and now my dream was going to become a reality sooner than I thought.

After the excitement wore off a little, I began to wonder how much an airline ticket would cost, and, in my ignorance, ventured to inquire. "Don't worry, buddy. We'll take care of everything." Orlando said with a smile. This was a huge relief to me, because I knew that my parents would not be able to fund such a trip, owing to the financial challenges they faced. Suddenly a new thought struck me – my father. Mom would surely give me permission to go on the trip, but would my father be so willing? I was not so sure about him giving his consent, as he was still not a Christian and might not understand the whole purpose of the trip.

About an hour later, I was surprised to see my mother, rather than my father, come to the bookstore to fetch me. She had just come from making purchases for our business and when she entered, the first thing she heard about was the trip. Praise God that Orlando had not yet left the shop; otherwise she would have thought I was joking! Indeed, everything seemed so surreal that even I felt as though I was half-dreaming. But, there I was, sitting with my mom, Orlando and his wife, Xiomara, talking about this great missionary adventure. Once all points had been discussed, my mother surprised me by saying that the Lord had already spoken to her, telling her that He was going to open doors in the nations very soon.

Mom gave her consent, but then she looked at me with slight uncertainty, saying, "What I don't know is what my husband is going to say about this. He doesn't believe the same way we do." Well, after those words, we prayed together for the trip and left. I was so excited I could not help but talk about it all the way home. When we arrived, the first thing my mother did was call my father to tell him all that had transpired.

"José, I have something to tell you," she said.

He interrupted her saying, "Yes, but first I have something to share with you." Intrigued, we let him begin. "You know that I am not a Christian or a believer in the things you believe in, but last night I had a vivid dream. I saw Alejandro at the airport saying goodbye to us. The only other thing I can remember is that he was going to preach abroad."

I could hardly believe what my ears were hearing – the Lord had already prepared my dad's heart for the conversation that we were going to have! When my father finished, I told him about Orlando's invitation to preach in Venezuela and asked if he would give me permission. Stunned by his experience, Dad gave me his consent without much thought. I was literally seeing God's hand in every detail of the trip, espccially in how He had touched both my parent's hearts. That in itself was a miracle.

Every detail, from clothes to my passport, was a continuous faith-adventure. This was my first international trip, and with it came many particulars that were miraculously facilitated and supplied by God's hand.

The Dream Becomes a Reality

During the first week of my stay in Guanare, Portuguesa (about 7 hours from Caracas), time was spent socializing, sightseeing and generally just having fun. Secretly, I felt disappointed, because I had no intention of going that far purely for enjoyment. Deep in my heart, I longed so badly to step up to a pulpit and preach the Gospel. Finally, Orlando invited all his family and some friends to a service one night. I was told I would give a word of encouragement after Orlando had sung a couple of Venezuelan songs. As many of Orlando's family were not yet saved, it was an exciting opportunity.

After praying, Orlando introduced me to the crowd as the boy preacher. When I stepped up to the pulpit and opened my Bible, I suddenly felt like fire was streaming down my body! As soon as I opened my mouth, words filled with conviction began to pour out. God touched me so powerfully that the message lasted two and a half hours. (That was back in the day when I was a long-winded preacher who enjoyed yelling at the top of my lungs as other Pentecostal preachers did!) After the meeting, I invited everyone present to accept Christ.

Sadly though, even with the unusual circumstance of an eleven-year-old telling them how to live their lives according to the Gospel, some of Orlando's relatives felt they were doing just fine. Since his brothers were wealthy professionals and non-religious people, it was twice as hard to convince them of their true state – that there would always be a void in their lives as long as they didn't accept a relationship with Christ. After appealing to them for about 10 minutes, I suddenly heard someone weeping. To my surprise, it was Orlando's sister who had come forward after she felt convicted by the Holy Spirit. After that, I felt as though the ice broke and more folks came forward to repent of their sins. Some also received the Holy Spirit for the first time.

Days after this experience, I found myself praying again, "Lord, I didn't come here for a vacation. Please open more doors; I want to preach your Gospel." God, however, already had a preaching schedule in place for me during my stay in Guanare! Through word of mouth, He began to forge divine connections, which opened up the way for me. Things began to move quickly from preaching to my toys, Lego blocks and sister's teddy bears, to realizing the dream He had put in my heart. Indeed, it still felt like I was dreaming sometimes, especially when I preached live to hundreds or perhaps even thousands of people via radio.

Before long, pastors from all over the city began to invite me to share my testimony; my agenda became so hectic that some Sundays I would preach two or three services. The schedule was so intense that I reached the point where I wore myself out and, just three days before going back home, I had to cancel some engagements due to a severe cold. In spite of this, God truly showed up in those last few meetings where hundreds of people were touched by His power, and many souls surrendered their lives to Jesus. That time in Venezuela deeply impacted my life, leaving me with unforgettable memories; ones which would signify the beginning of a wonderful, supernatural journey.

After those four intense weeks, I returned home, very excited to see my family. It seemed much longer than it actually was, being my first missionary trip and given that I was just eleven, traveling without my parents. They came to pick me up from the airport and a happy family reunion followed. Life went on as usual and all returned to normal: church, homework and family. It seemed to me like I had emerged from a month-long dream and would perhaps never go back to Venezuela. There had been, after all, a sense of finality when I said goodbye to Orlando's family. Little did I know however, I would return to Venezuela many times in the years to come and that this was only the beginning of many international trips.

Chapter 11

What Should I Do Now That I Have Seen The Power Of God?

Back home, all my friends at school wanted to talk about was my trip. They asked me lots of questions, which surprised me at first and later turned out to be a fantastic opportunity to witness to them. There were also questions in my own mind at the time, such as, "Would I preach once again at the park? Would I travel again overseas? What should I do, now that I had seen the power of God first-hand?" Those questions lingered, until one day my pastor invited me to preach in his church and share what happened in Venezuela. Somehow, this opened the way for me to receive invitations from other local churches to speak, and so I continued to minister in this new capacity.

During my first week back in Costa Rica, it was also

time to catch up with all the homework I had missed. I thank God for my friends who helped me get up to speed. In spite of having not been to school for an entire month, God gave me favor and helped me pass my grade with remarkable scores, even helping me place second in my class. As God also gave me favor with my teachers, I was able to travel more and more. At the end of my travels, I would always catch up with my friends and update my books, copying out any missed lessons. I thank God that He gave me such understanding teachers, and that they were so very gracious to me during my final year of elementary school.

The Gala Night

It was almost the end of the school year and we were all preparing to have our school gala night. We were very excited, especially those of us who had a companion for the big night. I was just a bit radical for any of the girls to want to be my date, but that was fine with me. I dreaded girls and was quite reserved around them. Not that I had much interaction with them at school, apart from preaching to them. Even at recess, I had a very strict routine of going to my favorite spot to study the Scriptures. I was undertaking a discipleship course offered by my church, which meant trying to keep up with both my Bible studies and school studies.

At the gala night, a toast was offered to the students. We were each given a tiny bit of juice in the bottom of our plastic cups, some brief speeches were made, and we drank. As soon as I swallowed the liquid, I noticed that it tasted funny...and smelt a bit off. Later that evening, I learned that some of the parents serving at the ball thought it would be funny to put actual wine in our cups without letting us know. Having made a promise to the Lord not to drink alcohol, I was disgusted with myself. I felt furious with those who did it and very much convicted, but it was too late. I had already drunk the wine and was digesting it. When my friends found out, they thought it was particularly funny that "El Pastorcito" (Little Pastor) had drunk alcohol, knowing my distaste for it.

The atmosphere began to change for the worse after the wine incident. Some students discovered the wine's source and were sneaking more; progressively becoming tipsy. Consequently, their behavior began to deteriorate. It was sad, for example, to see many of my classmates dancing to music in an immoral way. By now, my desire to leave the party was so strong that I snuck out without letting anybody know and walked home.

On the brink of becoming a teenager, I was entering a new stage in my life, one that would test me in many different ways, which could potentially conflict with or distract me from my calling. I found that being a teen preacher proved even harder than being a child preacher. I thank God though that He guided me through those turbulent waters and safely into the harbor of adulthood, still serving Him.

Sometimes you may wonder if it possible to live in holiness in the midst of the world we live in. I would answer that question with a resounding, "Yes!" It is possible, as long as your drive to seek God is stronger than your drive to do worldly things. I know it is difficult, but trust me; God is the only one who can help us overcome those temptations. Remember, that Jesus was also a teenager and a young adult and that He went through similar circumstances – even growing up 2000 years ago in Bethlehem. He understands what we as youth go through every single day, because He died for our sins and through Him we receive redemption.

My Dad Surrenders His Life to Christ

The same year I graduated from elementary school, I began to receive invitations to preach all over Costa Rica. As I accepted them, God miraculously opened big doors for the ministry. This sometimes produced opposition, as some felt that I was too young to be given such opportunities. Yes, there was a high price to pay, but I was willing to do it, regardless of who criticized me or how many hours I had to ride on a bus through the mountains to get to a tiny village in the middle of nowhere. Every weekend I was ready, my bags packed, excited to head out on a wonderful adventure somewhere deep in Costa Rica. It was not a glamorous life; sometimes our experiences were tiring and difficult, especially during seasons when we were not reimbursed for our expenses.

My dad, José, and I were very new to the ministry life style and each trip was a steep learning curve. How ironic it was though, that even with Dad still an unbeliever, he was part of the ministry! He was very supportive of me and wanted to help me get started. I never thought we were going to be on the road every weekend like our neighbor, Leo, who was a traveling evangelist. He had been traveling for many years and he would often tell me how difficult it was.

After those first few months, my mom and dad began to take turns coming with me on mission trips. Unfortunately though, it eventually became too much for my mom and she became burnt out from so much travel on the weekends.

One night I heard my parents discuss whether I should continue traveling as an evangelist or go back to school and just be a regular kid. After their long conversation, my dad decided to continue traveling with me full time, although, he insisted on keeping the bar business open. My mom was unhappy about this as she had been praying for the bar to close down. In spite of it staying open and the subsequent disagreement between my parents, the Lord had everything under control. This became clear when He spoke to my dad one night in a dream, telling him to shut down his businesses. Dad broke the news to us the following morning, much to our surprise.

The enemy is never happy with such decisions, however, and opposition began to arise from a number of places, in particular, from Dad's own family. His parents were concerned that he hadn't made a wise decision and feared that he might no longer be able to provide for his family. Some of my dad's aunts and uncles also disagreed with the decision and criticized him harshly. As for my mom and me, we were very excited and happy to see his progress. Little by little, my dad began to surrender his heart as the Lord worked to soften and change it.

One night we went to San Vito, Coto Bruz, which is about 6 hours away from San José, Costa Rica's capital. When the service started, the Holy Spirit began to move powerfully. As I was preaching, I noticed that my dad had come into the church. This was unusual because he would normally stay outside listening to the message, but that night he sat in the back row. Before I made the altar call, I looked up and saw my dad with his head bowed and both arms resting on the back of the pew in front of him. Thinking he must be ill, I became worried, wondering what could be the matter. To my utter astonishment, when I gave the altar call, my dad was among the people who came forward to accept salvation. With tears streaming down his face, he knelt in front of the altar and prayed the sinner's prayer. The senior pastor, (who had been watching the entire scene in amazement), helped my dad fill out a response card.

That night, an ordinary service became a revival meeting, which lasted for five hours! It was an awesome celebration of dancing and worshipping God, with many people being healed. The most wonderful miracle of all for me, however, was my father's salvation that night.

A Baptism Miracle

After the beautiful time we spent in San Vito, we returned home, where my dad faced some big decisions. The most important (and hardest) one was to completely let the Holy Spirit manage his life. As a new believer, he had to learn to take his first steps as a Christian, learning how to live and act like Christ. This meant letting go of any addictions. Surprisingly, alcohol, his strongest vice, was relatively easy for him to let go of. There was another one, however, that proved more stubborn.

Suddenly, my dad was aware that he was going to have to let go of his nightly habit of smoking a cigarette before hitting the sack. His custom was to go outside in the dark, light a cigarette and stay there smoking pensively for a few minutes. This was designed so that no one, including my mother, would be aware of what he was doing. That is, until one night when a pastor caught him smoking in his backyard. Seeing the pastor, my dad was embarrassed; he tossed the cigarette to the ground and went to bed. Even though the pastor knew my dad had recently become a Christian, this didn't seem to help matters; he never invited us back to his church.

My dad prayed hard after this experience that God would release him from his twenty-year habit, but still found that he couldn't go to sleep without his nightly cigarette. As our home church's baptisms drew near, he grew concerned about the idea of being baptized. He decided to make a special request to God – that he would be set free from his addiction from the moment he was baptized. Sure enough, God answered his prayer supernaturally. The day after being baptized my dad tried, (out of curiosity), to light up a cigarette and see what would happen. Every nerve in his body rejected the smell of the smoke, and he has never lit up another cigarette since.

Traveling Companions

My dad and I became good travel companions and went to as many places as the Lord led us. From small towns to big cities, from preaching to farmers to praying for business men and women, from the capital city to the borders of Costa Rica, from preaching to small crowds to packed venues, we saw God move mightily. As we crisscrossed Costa Rica, God suddenly began to open doors for us to travel to other Central American nations: Nicaragua, Panama, and Guatemala. Packing and unpacking bags quickly became something of a weekend hobby for me. As more and more invitations came in, my parents began to take turns traveling with me once more. I dearly thank God for the wonderful, brave and supportive parents He gave me, parents who often made great sacrifices so the ministry could continue reaching the nations for Christ.

Needless to say, criticism from both sides of my family was ongoing from those who still disagreed with my parents' deep commitment to the ministry. Some close family members told my dad that spending time traveling wasn't going to cover the bills. The pressure began to mount, especially when, after a crusade in Cariari (about two and a half hours from San José), we found ourselves without enough money to get us back home.

God provided supernaturally, and we managed to make it back. Upon our return, piled-up bills awaited us on the kitchen table (which was becoming something of a pattern.) My mom had finally had enough and said she couldn't continue going on the way we had, living only by faith. This deeply saddened my heart.

After a few hours of discussion, my parents decided it was time to make a turnaround for the better and change the way we had been managing the ministry.

Up till that moment, all I had known was the taste of living by faith and knowing that our provision came from God! I was so blessed every time we saw God move in this particular issue. He blessed us and surprised us every weekend and every miracle we saw was like another faith-shot that kept us going, right up until this most recent event.

Depending on God Alone

God likes it when we truly depend on Him and stop thinking about our plan B or C. Those plans are most likely to invade our minds when we are going through challenges in life. However, it is always better to opt for the Lord's plan. Remember, His ways are higher than ours. Also remember that the God of Israel is watching your back and He will never let you down. Depending on God is as necessary as depending on the air we breathe to survive each day. We can depend on other devices to live, like breathing machines, but they are a poor substitute for the most mysterious thing God created – air. I say "mysterious," because we feel air but never see it.

> "The wind blows wherever it pleases. You hear its sound, but you cannot tell where it comes from or where it is going. So it is with everyone born of the Spirit." John 3:8 (NIV)

That is how we must also live by faith – trusting that what we cannot see will be brought into being to sustain us.

> "Now faith is the substance of things hoped for, the evidence of things not seen." Hebrews 11:1 (KJV)

Dependency on God has to be our primary source of survival in this adventure we live each day. We need to believe by faith that He will bring the rushing winds that divide the waters, so that we can cross to the other side of our challenges, walking into our destiny! All we need to do is hold on tightly to His promises and breath them in and allowing them to sustain us – even in life's toughest seasons. Depending on God is not easy, but it is the most powerful choice we believers can make in our daily lives. It should also be our only option. We need to be like eagles, positioning ourselves to catch the "tailwind" of God's provision and power, which will carry us forward. As sensitive as an eagle is to the winds, so we must also trust God and be sensitive to His leading in our lives.

The more we depend on God, the more sensitive we become to His presence, and the more obedient we become, the better choices we make. Even when we feel like no wind is blowing and we are suffocated by the heat of our circumstances, that is when we need to trust Him the most.

A Gift

I recall another occasion when we were on the road, with just enough money for the bus tickets home. Strangely enough in the face of such circumstances, I found myself craving a packet of potato chips and a strawberry milkshake. While I was riding on the bus, thinking about what I could do with my spare time, I felt the sudden prompt to preach to the passengers. God honored his Word, even on the bus, and many people were touched by the Spirit. Some of them were even crying at the back and ended up surrendering their lives to Christ. This occasion was very special and unusual. Although over the years I had become accustomed to preaching the Gospel on a bus, something happened I had never seen before: conviction, repentance and ultimately revival broke out in the bus that day.

We were chatting with some believers after we got off the bus when suddenly a lady approached me and, with a big smile, placed something in my hand. When she walked away, I opened my hand and found there another beautiful gift God had lavished on me! It was the exact amount I needed to buy the snacks I had been craving. Those were the kind of moments that kept me going and believing that everything was going to be all right! Whether it was a small gift to cover a meal, or an unexpected check in the mail to cover some of our ministry expenses, God always provided for us.

Today, I invite you to believe in God for supernatural provision! I have always believed that when God gives a vision, He also gives the provision. This is exactly what I have witnessed on every single trip, even up until this very day.

Chapter 12

A Youngster In Bible School

As I traveled more in Costa Rica and the neighboring nations, I began to believe that God wanted me to focus on the ministry full-time, and that He wanted me to focus on His Kingdom affairs rather than spending my time doing anything else. This was confirmed when the opportunity came along for me to study at a renowned Bible school in San José.

I had been longing to attend the college and enroll in their intensive Biblical Studies course, so I was delighted that a door had been opened for me there. One day, my mom and I went to the college to check out the premises and inquire about the pre-requisites for my course. It happened that while we were there, we also bumped into the school Dean, whom I had only seen on TV. When I asked him if I could have a minute of his time, he smiled kindly and replied that I could have five. I told him what I had in mind, and asked if he would consider admitting me as a student to the college, in spite of my age. He said he had heard of me but could not promise anything because of the age requirement for admittance into the school. I suddenly felt embarrassed. Here I was, only twelve-years-old, talking to the director and asking him to admit me into one of the most popular Bible schools in San José. To my surprise though, he said, "Okay, I will make a deal with you. Go back home and pray about this. If I call you, then unfortunately it will be to let you know you haven't been accepted, but, if you *don't* hear from me, then you will know you have been admitted."

The following day, I submitted my ministry resume and some letters of recommendation. A week went by and no one called from IBCS. I went to the school at the start of the semester, excited but also a little nervous, lest I had missed their phone call and had actually been turned away. It was a huge relief when I saw my name on the list of newly enrolled students! I was over the moon and so excited that I proceeded to shake everyone's hand and introduced myself to all of the teachers. I was perhaps a little too bold and confident for a kid, and from time to time some of the adult students and even some of the teachers suggested that I was too young to be there or that I was wasting my youth by not enjoying my childhood. I was taken aback, never having felt for one second that I was throwing my youth away. On the contrary, I was very happy to have been called by God at such an early age.

It was a long, intensive, yet rewarding seven months at the Bible school, and I thank God for all my Bible teachers – particularly for my mentor, Apostle Rony Chaves. He taught me many things that helped me mature in the ministry. In July 2001, at the age of thirteen, I graduated from Bible College with several of my friends and classmates. The day that the ceremony was held, my family and I had been out on our grandparent's farm, about 60km from San José. We were planning to catch the bus back for the ceremony until a providential turn of events took place. It so happened that a very well known Christian Senator, Mr. Justo Orozco, was in Guapiles for the day, speaking at a Christian rally. When we bumped into him and he found out that we would soon be heading back to San José for my college graduation ceremony, he offered to give us a ride in his private government car. Years later, God would again call upon this kind-hearted man to assist me, this time by providing me with letters to the American Embassy, thus helping me obtain my first visa into the United States.

Chapter 13

Walking In The Supernatural

It had been almost a year since God had called me into full-time ministry and more doors were opening by the day. I saw that God began to expedite many things in our ministry, and that He was swiftly equipping us in order to be more efficient in His work. In spite of this, in my own personal walk with the Lord, I felt as though I was at a plateau. Even with all that was going on around me, I wasn't quite content. I wanted to see more of God. I knew there was more to my calling than just preaching. There was something greater and deeper than I had yet to see with my eyes. As a teen preacher, I became very hungry to learn more about the supernatural and became desperate to experience it in a greater measure. At this point in our ministry, we had witnessed miracles every now and then, but I wanted oh so much more of God! There had to be more of His presence and power than what I was experiencing!

One weekend, I was invited to preach in Playa Dominical (Dominical Beach) and as I was getting my bags ready for the long trip, I felt a prompting in my heart to grab a book off the shelf. The book was *Good Morning, Holy Spirit* by Pastor Benny Hinn. I wanted to feed my spirit during the 5-hour bus ride. While I was reading, I began to pray and sing softly. That day, my dad was traveling with me and he sat on my left. A lady sat to my right, and, as I began to chat with her, I realized she was a Christian. What a joyous trip that was, we both sang and prayed all along the way! By the end of the trip, the people in the bus had probably figured out that we were two "crazy" Christians!

As I mentioned, I had been praying for a while before this trip, hoping to see a breakthrough in our ministry. I sensed that something special was going to happen this weekend. When we got off the bus, a pastor welcomed us and took us to his house. We had a snack and got ready for the meeting. When we arrived, I observed that the atmosphere was quite dull and cold. When I got up to speak, I could feel heaviness in the air – almost tangibly, and every word that came out of my mouth was empty, as though it were being sucked into deep space. I felt completely inadequate and very much longed to leave that place. I came to a point, however, when I was standing there on the platform preaching my lungs out, when I decided to surrender myself to the Lord. I had no strength left and I felt extremely disappointed. Everyone had been anticipating that something great was going to happen. Surely that would be the case with all the built-up expectation for the event, all the advertising and having several pastors come together in unity with prayer and fasting. No one could understand why there was now such pressure and such opposition in the Spirit.

I was wrapping up the message and ready to make the altar call when a sense of fear and uncertainty swept over me. I froze, wondering just what really was going on. For a few brief moments no one responded. Then suddenly, I heard a cry and I opened my eyes to see a weeping child running toward the stage. He was shouting praises to God, saying that he'd just experienced a miracle. He gave his testimony, telling how he'd been healed in his spine and that all the pain had left his body. After this, all heaven broke loose and revival rains flooded down on us. Later that night, we heard as many as thirty testimonies of healing. Lots of people came forward and were prayed over, and many received the baptism of the Holy Spirit. What an amazing service it was and what a glorious way to kick off the crusade!

The following morning, the Holy Spirit woke me up. I was trying to pray and to stay awake, when suddenly I saw an angel. My whole body shook; I had seen angels in the past, but this one was quite big and strong - a warrior angel, carrying a fiery sword with him. He spoke to me, and showed me how the city was filled with witchcraft. As I grasped the vision, the angel asked me to grab a pen and to write down the plan of attack that we were going to undertake.

Hours later, my father and I went down to the church and participated in a day of fasting. After we prayed, God confirmed the same strategy the angel had given me to some of the intercessors in the church. At the end of the day, we ended up at the big soccer field where the next meeting was to be held and did a prayer march, going around it seven times.

That night, we all felt as though something had been

broken in the spiritual realm. The place was filled with the presence of God and His glory became thicker and thicker as we worshipped Him. We could all feel that the atmosphere was much lighter. It was as though there was no more opposition from the evil one. After I preached for thirty minutes, the power of God was released and, at the altar call, more than eighty souls came forward before the Lord. When I looked at the number of people that responded to the altar call, my heart was filled with joy and gratitude for what the Lord had done. What an awesome night that was! At the end, some of the local pastors told us that they had never seen such a harvest of souls in one meeting. From that day on, I began to walk in the supernatural with God!

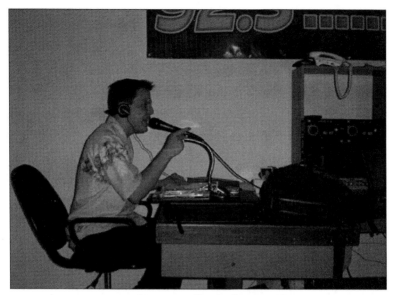

Preaching on radio, Aruba, age 17.

Healing crusade in Medellin, Colombia, age 18.

Youth rally in Madras, India, at New Life Assembly of God, 2008.

Healing meeting in Mayaguez, Puerto Rico, 2009.

Conference at Faith Christian Outreach Church, Mount Pleasant.

Daystar TV interview, in the USA.

TBN Enlace TV interview, in Costa Rica.

Rebekah and me on our wedding day in Perth, Australia, June 25th, 2011.

Chapter 14

Activate Your Dreams

God is faithful to fulfill the promises He has given us for our lives. However, there is also a condition: We must activate these dreams by a willingness to step out in faith. Our dreams will not be activated until we begin to walk in the direction God has called us to. It is necessary to follow God's compass and walk in His will in order to enter the promised destiny. We must not simply "name it and claim it" as the popular Christian slogan goes, but also act upon the dreams God has given us, remembering that,

> "…faith by itself, if it is not accompanied by action, is dead." James 2:17

Do not let fear hold you back! Step out of the boat as Peter did, and walk towards Jesus and towards the destiny He has for your life. Do not be afraid of the risk of failure. Many times, when we hear a sermon preached about Peter walking on the water, the emphasis is upon his "failure." When Peter became afraid he began to sink. Yes, it is true that sometimes failures occur in our lives, particularly if we take our eyes off our Lord Jesus, but there is also another lesson to be learned here. Even though Peter grew afraid when he was on the water, he was actually quite courageous even to get out of the boat in the first place, something that none of the other disciples dared to do! Not only that, Jesus' invitation to Peter to come to Him on the water was preceded by Peter's bold request:

> "Lord, if it's you...tell me to come to you on the water." (Matthew 14:28)

In a sense, it was as if Peter was unwittingly saying to Jesus, "Challenge me, Lord – if that's really you, I should be able to walk on the water too in your power! Move me out of my comfort zone! Take me out into the unknown!" For us, the "boat" in our lives may represent our comfort zones, the everyday and the norm, the routines we can become stuck in- day in and day out. Such a life is only half-lived. Indeed, without faith we do not truly live but rather we "do" life. We do not truly live because we do not aspire to a full life of seeing our dreams come true!

There is more! God has a plan for your life and it speaks directly to your own sense of purpose and fulfillment. His plan will not only bring fulfillment, it will touch the lives of others as you draw closer to Him.

I believe that in these last days, God is calling His children to step out of the boat as Peter did. It is time for us to step out of the "boat" of our own comfort and out into the sea of humanity, where we can identify with the cold hard, realities of what others are facing – the realities of a dying world. As we draw closer to the heart of Jesus, our hearts should too go out to the orphans, the poor, the widows and the hurting. Much of the Word of God reads like a love letter to such people. If we truly have our hearts beating in time with His, we will love those He loves and we will be willing to have our hearts broken for the things that break His, such as injustice and oppression. Through loving others, we will know more about His love.

We need not be afraid to fail, as God promises that,

"...in all things [He] works for the good of those who love Him, who have been called according to His purpose." Romans 8:28

Fear only causes us to miss God and to lose divine opportunities that come our way. If we focus on fear, we are in fact focusing on our own human frailty and ourselves. But if we keep our eyes fixed on Christ, we will see His promises come to fruition!

We must do as James encourages us,

"If any of you lacks wisdom, he should ask God, who gives generously to all without finding fault, and it will be given to him." James 1:5 (NIV)

Do you trust God enough to let Him guide you? Do you trust Him enough to believe that even if you miss His leading and begin to "sink," He will reach out and pull you up? We can step out onto the water with confidence, remembering God's promise in Isaiah 43:2, "When you pass through the waters, I will be with you; and when you pass through the rivers, they will not sweep over you." (NIV)

Allow fear to drive you closer to Jesus, rather than away from him. Instead of being ashamed of your fears, let them cause you to cry out, "Lord, I need you!"

If you have surrendered your life fully to Christ, and have told Him that you are willing to chase His dreams for you, (in spite of how uncomfortable it may be), He will not let you down – even if you make a mistake somewhere along the line. He will even turn your experience into a lesson, which will serve you well, bringing you to the next level. This is part of the very necessary refining process we must undergo if we are to see the fulfillment of God's dreams for us.

If we do not undergo a process before we step into the fullness of God's destiny for us, tragedy can occur. For example, we see this time and time again when young people in Hollywood achieve too much, too soon. They achieve success, but lack the character to sustain it with integrity. Over time, their own successes can actually end up destroying them. In the same way, if we are not willing to go through the refining process, there is a danger that we can begin to think we achieved success through our own human efforts. There is also the subtle danger of beginning to glorify the dreams of God above Him. The fulfillment of His dreams in our life should always have one goal – to glorify Him and lift His Name high.

We need to allow God to transform our human thinking, until we understand that total dependency is the key to achieving greatness in God. If we dream dreams that are achievable only in our own strength, there is a good chance that such dreams are not of God. If our dreams are made of the impossible, however, (with no way for them to come through apart from God's hand), then we will see His glory!

Along this journey, there have been many experiences God has given me, which I now recognize as being part of His blueprint for my life. Each event, big or small, bears the mark of His divine fingerprint. Dear friend, such events and experiences can only encourage and build our faith, helping us trust more in God and step out of our "boats." Therefore, activate your dreams!

Chapter 15

Disappointments And Trials

It was the National Day of Prayer, when all the churches gathered to pray for Costa Rica. I used to love such prayer rallies. They were a lot of fun, especially when I got hold of a bunch of tracts and passed them out in the crowd. This day was different, however. I was seated at the front with other ministers in the reserved seating, which meant I couldn't take off passing out tracts like before! I sat for a while, observing the crowds slowly packing the stadium, filing in from every corner of Costa Rica, carrying their home-made placards and banners. Some people had already begun praying, and the low buzz of their prayers charged the atmosphere with an electric excitement. The rally had not even begun and the presence of God was descending on the people!

Before long, I noticed a friend of mine sitting on the platform. Deciding to risk a quick hello, I made my way towards him. As I did so, I was confronted with a veritable wall of ushers and security personnel surrounding the platform. Security was high, as Senator Orazco would be speaking. It looked nearly impossible to get past them, until God supernaturally intervened. My friend, Pastor Javier Espinoza, spotted me and motioned for me to come up. He told an usher that I was a friend and, before I knew it, I was standing on the platform among some of the Christian leaders of the day whom I most admired! For a thirteen-year-old just getting started in ministry, this was tremendously exciting.

After we chatted a few minutes, Javier asked me if I wanted to meet Pastor Steve Fatow, from the US. For a moment, the name sounded familiar, and I suddenly realized that he was none other than the keynote speaker. Javier had coordinated his involvement in the event. I was very excited and replied that I would love to meet Pastor Steve.

I had, in fact, seen him preach a couple of years back and had prayed a prayer so fleeting that it was little more than a thought: "What an anointed servant of God. Lord, I would love to meet him somehow." God had heard my prayer however, and now here I was, about to receive the fulfillment of that dream.

In my broken English, I said, "Hello" and shook Pastor Steve's hand. He asked me a few questions, but since I couldn't quite grasp what he was saying, my friend Javier intervened and interpreted for us. Pastor Steve prayed for me after we spoke, saying to Javier, "I would very much like to have this young boy at my church, please make sure you help him out." As I stood there between them, Pastor Javier took me by the hand and said something I will never forget: "God will do amazing things with you, brother."

With the rally about to begin, I said, "Goodbye" and went back to my seat.

Almost a year went by and no official invitation came, not even an email or a phone call. There were times when I thought all had been forgotten. Every day I would pray, thinking about Pastor Steve's words and continue to dream that one day God would open the doors of that great nation, the United States of America. It was disappointing to have to wait, but if I could have seen the future, I would have realized that one day God would bring this all to pass, and more. He *would* be glorified.

Among God's greatest attributes is His faithfulness! Through the tests and trials, through the waiting and character building, our Heavenly Father is always there to dry our tears and give us a hug. Some may think that working in ministry is easy. But there is a price to pay. Sometimes we are required to wait. Our job, in the meantime, is to simply be like clay in His precious hands, allowing Him to mold our character. Only then can we grow in faith and become instruments of His glory. Even Jesus Christ, the very Son of God, was required to wait and was tested. For thirty years He completed his pre-ministerial training, before being led to the wilderness to be tempted by the devil. After passing the three tests the devil presented him,

> "...Jesus returned to Galilee in the power of the Spirit, and news about Him spread through the whole countryside." Luke 4:14 (NIV)

This sequence of events illustrates how each test in our

lives is geared up by the Lord to result in a victory. Only *after* Jesus successfully completed His wilderness assignment, could He go to the next level. Jesus' endurance resulted in promotion, and His triumph over trials resulted receiving a greater endowment of God's power. Therefore, we must allow the Lord to use challenges and periods of waiting in our lives to produce a greater manifestation of His power.

We will face our trials in life, but there *will* be promotion. After your wilderness, there is a promised land waiting for you, my friend! So don't ever give up, but continue running the race – your reward is at hand. God honors those who honor Him!

When God began to use me, He also began to mold me. There was a period of formation in my life which seemed slow at times. Sometimes, I wondered why I couldn't just get down to business right away, but then God reminded me,

> "Whoever can be trusted with very little can also be trusted with much." Luke 16:10 (NIV)

I learned that in order to protect the dream-seed God had given me; I needed to nurture it with the words of my mouth. The Scriptures teach us that there is power in our confession. Concerning the influence of words, the Apostle James wrote,

> "When we put bits into the mouths of horses to make them obey us, we can turn the whole animal." James 3: 3 (NIV)

In the same way, our words can direct the very course of

our lives. Confessing our dreams is a way of activating them in faith and believing that God will fulfill them.

We need to prophesy over our circumstances, speaking in faith, even when the outlook does not seem very promising. In this way, we tell our circumstances to get in line with our God-given destiny. We should not only be dreamers and speakers, however, but also *doers* of our Heavenly Father's will. In this way, we will see the fulfillment of those dreams. If we believe God will do what He has promised, we must act upon it.

We must also have the faith necessary to overcome obstacles along the way. This is the example the "Heroes of the Faith" have shown us in the Word. They were required to make radical decisions, in various ways, in order to walk in alignment with God's plan. The classic example given for us is that of Abraham, who left his country and family, without knowing where he was going (Hebrews 11:8). With no GPS or map book, Abraham's conviction led him out into the desert and into the will of the Almighty.

There are moments when we need to make challenging decisions in order to advance in the perfect will of God. Remember, strive not only to have a dream or vision, but also strive to see its fulfillment. This is the time for you to not only dream, but also to take the steps necessary to enter a new level. As you do so, however, never lose sight of the fact that it is ultimately God who promotes us and brings us to the Promised Land. It is not by our own strength but by His Holy Spirit,

"'Not by might nor by power, but by my Spirit,' says the Lord Almighty." Zechariah 4:6 (NIV)

Furthermore, God honors His children's obedience. Obedience accelerates the process He wants to do in our lives, and takes us to places we could not imagine. If we walk in the direction of His Spirit, we will certainly reach the place of our destiny. If we leave His will, on the other hand, it could cost us a very high price. Doing so can cause considerable setbacks, or even the loss of a dream. We must be led by the cloud of God's guiding presence and follow His plan to the letter.

Chapter 16

The Dream-Killers

From a very young age, I always had the conviction that God had a great calling for my life, but from time to time "dream-killers" would arise – those who did not believe that God would call a child from such a young age.

An incident which comes to mind stems from my liking of prayer, intercession and spiritual warfare as a youngster. I would often shut myself away in my room to engage in such activities, playing my praise and worship tapes. One day, after a particularly energetic prayer session, a worried neighbor called my mother to warn her that engaging in spiritual warfare could in fact cause the enemy to attack me. She'd apparently "heard from the Lord" – that my mother should advise me to stop! Unfortunately though, my mom was a new Christian and didn't understand what the neighbor was talking about.

While listening to the Christian radio station that afternoon, she heard a pastor answering questions and giving biblical counsel. Suddenly it dawned on her, here was the chance to clear up any doubts. Immediately, she dialed the radio station's number and mentioned the morning's incident.

I remember hearing all this going on from my room and thinking, "Lord, please may my neighbor hear this." The pastor on the other end of the phone then said, "Tell this sister that the only one who should shut up is the enemy, because there is power in prayer!" From that day on, the neighbor did not make any more remarks about my prayer life!

I also learned over the years (sometimes the hard way), the importance of only sharing God-given dreams to other like-minded visionaries. Doing so ensures that we will be built up by mutual encouragement, rather than be disheartened by negative counsel. If you share your dreams with the wrong people, the enemy can use that to try to discourage you, embitter you, and ultimately get you off track. Sharing dreams with the wrong people is how negative criticism can arise and how envy is cultivated, resulting in disagreements. Before speaking, we need to use the twin spiritual weapons God has given us, of discernment and wisdom.

On other occasions, it was fierce gossip that tested me. Comments such as, I was naïve, I was too young to be serious, it was just a phase – I heard all this and more from those skeptical of my calling. After hearing such things, I would go into the restroom and cry, often asking God, "Why?" From time to time, someone would warn my parents that when I hit my youth, I would fall in love with a girl, and all this "emotion" would dissipate. Deep in my heart, however, I sensed that the calling of God wasn't going to stop when I turned thirteen – or any other age, for that matter.

It was also difficult to find good mentors. There were some men who wanted me to emulate them and follow their example. The problem was that they were not walking righteously before the Lord. I longed for strong, honorable mentors to encourage and lead me; but instead I was often met with discouragement.

In those days, I continued to watch "This Is Your Day," and read books by Benny Hinn. I learned a lot about the Holy Spirit through his materials. On one particular occasion, I was enjoying his program when the pastor I was staying with asked me, "What are you watching?" I replied, "Benny Hinn." The pastor walked over to the television and abruptly turned it off. He looked at me and said sternly, "You will never achieve such things!" I was utterly speechless. Later that night, I shut myself in my prayer closet and poured out my pain to the Lord.

Dream-killers never encourage. They will rob you of your dreams. One example from the Bible of dream-killers in action can be found in Numbers 13. Here we find the account of the Israelite spies sent into Canaan. At the end of 40 days, they returned to the Israelite camp at Kadesh in the desert of Paran, giving Moses and Aaron their report and showing the fruit of the land they had brought back. They told Moses, "We went into the land to which you sent us, and it does flow with milk and honey! Here is its fruit. But the people who live there are powerful and the cities are fortified and very large. We saw even the descendants of Anak there. The Amalekites live in the Negev; the Hittites, Jebusites and Amorites live in the hill country; and the Canaanites live near the sea and along the

Jordan." Numbers 13: 27-29 (NIV)

At times, we will have to face people, and even ministries, which will try and deter us from taking possession of all that God has promised. You can be encouraged, however, by the many godly men and women in the Bible who were faced with "Small Vision Syndrome." Caleb and Joshua were two such men. When the other spies said, "It can't be done," they replied, "We should go up and take possession of the land, for we can certainly do it." (Numbers 13:30) There was no question in Caleb and Joshua's minds that with God's help, anything was possible.

On many occasions, we as visionaries, are going to have to listen to one opinion alone – that of our Lord Jesus Christ! If we listen to what the dream-killers tell us, it can be dangerous, even abortive, for our dreams. Do not allow anything or anyone to discourage you, distract you or make you lose your focus. Walk beneath God's cloud and follow it, and the God of Abraham, Isaac and Jacob will show you His glory as you journey towards the Promised Land.

Don't expect everyone to recognize or acknowledge what God has placed in your heart. Sometimes, it may even be someone in a position of God-given authority over you who do not understand. Although this is a difficult situation, it does not give us the right to fly in the face of authority. Sadly, there are many who will go from church to church, causing divisions, bitterly defending their dreams and fighting vehemently against anyone they see as being "an obstacle" to them. Therefore, be prayerful and wise, avoiding the pitfalls. It is also important for us to respect spiritual authority, regardless of whether our dreams and callings are understood or not.

Remember, when Peter tried to turn Jesus aside from His calling, Jesus did not rebuke Peter, but Satan, the spirit operating against the will of God. For this reason, Jesus told Satan, rather than Peter, to get behind Him. Even if people are in opposition to you, remember that your fight is not against flesh and blood. (Ephesians 6:12) We must not attack people, but rather, pray against the spiritual forces trying to hinder God's will. Many times, people who discourage others do not even realize they are doing it. They think they are simply giving helpful counsel or "realistic" warnings. If your dream is of God, He will bring it to pass, regardless of whether those in positions of influence in your life believe in it or not. Knowing this prevents us from getting into conflicts and trying to defend ourselves in the flesh. Rest in God.

For your dreams to be realized, you will have to strike out in faith. But first, be absolutely certain that God is calling you to do what you have set out to achieve. God is your ultimate authority. If you do find yourself in a situation of conflict with a spiritual authority, remember to always deal with leadership in a respectful and loving way.

> "With all lowliness and meekness, with long-suffering, forbearing one another in love; endeavoring to keep the unity of the Spirit in the bond of peace." Ephesians 4:2, 3 (KJV)

Ask God to show you the way, as it is important that you be accountable. There are no lone rangers in the Kingdom of heaven. Even the pastors of the largest churches in the world need someone they can also call "Pastor;" someone they can go to for counsel and encouragement. Ask God to guide you to the right spiritual leader or leaders who can support you in fulfilling the call He has placed on your life.

Chapter 17

Expanding The Vision

From small farm towns to big cities and everything in between, we saw revival breaking out everywhere. Sometimes there were services that lasted 4-5 hours. As God expanded the vision, we received invitations to preach not only in church venues, but also in soccer fields, dance clubs, gyms and even bull fighting rings. Revival was not limited to church buildings! I remember another campaign we had in San Vito. The power of God was so intense that, despite the torrential rains, no one left the park. At one meeting, more than 100 souls came to Christ. As the Lord gave us favor, opportunities also came to share His Word in many national secular radio/TV stations, as well as in Christian media. The ministry was going through one of its "growth spurts" and it was amazing to see what the Lord was doing in such a short period of time!

During the filming of a television program, the Lord gave me the privilege of meeting a pastor I had seen in the past and had admired for his devotion and passion for serving the Lord.

Pastor William Magaña and I kept in touch, and he invited us to visit to his church. "Pasion por Las Almas" (Passion for Souls) had grown to become one of the largest churches in San José. I felt very humbled and excited to accept his invitation. That night when we arrived, Pastor William made sure we had a special seat in one of the guest rows. I was honored when, after he preached, he requested that I pray for the children and for the youth. "Pasion por las Almas" became my home church, and Pastor William became a dear friend to me.

In the quest of looking for a mentor, God had led me to the right person. He allowed me to stay by Pastor Magaña's side for many years, being trained and nurtured by him. "Pasion por las Almas," became a place of "refueling" for my family and I after long ministry. It was a place I felt I could return to and be refreshed. I remained working with Pastor William right up until the time I left Costa Rica to live overseas. I thank God for placing such a wonderful mentor in my life, one who not only helped shape me with his teaching but one who also blessed my ministry in many ways.

At the end of October in 2003, I was invited to preach at one of the largest churches in Costa Rica. I had long dreamt of doing so and had prayed for the Lord to open this door, but it didn't happen until His perfect time. It had come about when I was at a birthday party and had prayed for an elderly lady to be healed. What I didn't know was that her son was the pastor of this church. Touched by the prayer, they invited me to preach the following Sunday. As I went to leave the party, Pastor Vargas put his arm around me and said, "See you next week, Son." A few months later, when I got to know him more, I realized that this was his usual way of addressing young men or disciples – like a father would address his child. I liked that Pastor Vargas had a father's heart and felt a special connection with him.

The following Sunday came, cold and pouring down with rain. This type of weather is typical for Costa Rica, especially around August, when it is the middle of the wet season. This is especially true in the highlands of Moravia, the district where the church is located. My friend, Evelyn, drove me there that day, as it was her home church. Evelyn's children attended the church's school, and some afternoons my parents would drop me off at their house to play. This was probably an effort on their part to help me become more sociable with children my own age, but I am afraid to say that this notion backfired. Evelyn's house was full of all kinds of nooks and crannies, which, for me, meant that it resembled a giant prayer closet. I loved praying at Evelyn's house, continuing to develop my relationship with the Holy Spirit. Thank goodness, Evelyn understood this, being a passionate intercessor and a worshipper herself. She also had considerable knowledge of spiritual warfare and took me along with her to a number of prophetic conferences and Christian events. This was an amazing blessing for me and provided a time of intensive preparation. I thank God for Evelyn and for how she allowed God to use her in my spiritual training.

Somehow the ushers helped get us into the building without getting soaked and we were taken into the auditorium, where Pastor Vargas received us. He smiled and nodded, pointing to our seats. I turned around for a moment during the worship time and was overwhelmed by the thousands of people behind me. It was truly a beautiful thing to witness – to see so many people gathered in a church, worshiping God so passionately. The sound was truly impressive. It was like a dream – I wanted to pinch myself!

When I was called to the front, my legs were trembling. I had never before preached to a crowd this size, approximately five thousand. Praise God though, a few minutes into the sermon the anointing fell, and in an instant I felt all fear and nerves leave me! After I had preached for thirty minutes, the spirit of conviction suddenly came upon the place. When it came time for the altar call, many came forward to receive Jesus as their personal Savior.

I had little experience praying for people during the ministration time at that stage, so I hesitated for a moment, unsure how to proceed with the service. Pastor Vargas and some of his associates came up on the stage and were extending their hands towards the multitude. I decided to go down and lay hands on a few people, but returned to the platform when I didn't see much happening. I began to worry, asking myself, "How am I going to wrap up this service?" In the midst of my pondering and worrying, however, the Holy Spirit stopped me, asking me if I was going to let Him handle it. After repenting and asking the Lord to forgive me for being so overawed by the crowd, I proceeded to pray once more for the people.

As I did so, I saw a frail, elderly woman near the front in a wheelchair, raising her hands and worshipping God with all her heart. The Lord told me to go and pray for her, so I went down the stairs and approached her. If God was indeed going to heal her, it would take a lot of faith – I had never before prayed for anyone in a wheelchair.

I later learned that she had been wheelchair-bound for almost twenty-nine years. Remembering the words of Jesus and the power of confession, I asked her if she wanted to be healed. Immediately she opened her eyes, squeezed my hand and declared that she had been waiting for her miracle for a long time. As I began to pray for her, I could literally feel the anointing flow through her body and then suddenly it happened – she was there in front of me, standing on both feet.

Not satisfied, she said with a look of intense faith that she was ready to walk. You can imagine how the crowd erupted with praise and joyful applause to the Lord that night! The TV cameras were fixed on the lady and everyone held their breath, waiting for her to walk. Before I knew it, she was already moving forward. I took her by the hand to help her, but quickly realized she needed nothing of the sort. She let go of my hand and praised God that she had been healed. That was it – before the ushers could do anything, she was off and actually *running* across the platform. Back and forth she went, shouting, crying and running, giving glory to God.

After that incredible display of God's power, the multitude's faith rose and hundreds were healed of sicknesses. Countless testimonies were given and many people experienced the Holy Spirit for the first time. The service was extended well into the night. Pastor Vargas, who had to attend another meeting somewhere else, ended up giving the church keys to one of the ushers and asked him to close up when we had finished. Praise God for all that He did that glorious evening! Two months later, we heard from the lady who had been healed of paralysis, saying that she was exercising and feeling better than ever!

Chapter 18

Open Doors And A Foiled Plot

One day, the telephone rang. I was surprised to hear my Aunt Maria on the other end. She had moved to Nashville, Tennessee, about twenty years earlier and owned a Day Care Center, as well as being a columnist for the local paper. From time to time, she would come to visit us in Costa Rica and would always bring big boxes with her, stuffed with gifts and clothes to give away to the less fortunate. She had a nickname in the family, "Mother Teresa." Her kindness and her generous spirit always brought great happiness to our family. While I was talking to her that day, she suddenly asked me, "Alejandro, what is your biggest dream this year?"

I was thrown by the unexpected question, and found myself needing a few seconds to think about my reply. Taking a deep breath, I told her about one of my greatest dreams – to preach the Gospel in the United States of America. When I mentioned that a pastor from Knoxville had invited me; she interrupted me by saying, "Alex, that city isn't too far from Nashville." Although we didn't continue to speak of it much for the rest of the conversation, I had a sense that God was beginning to move the pieces of the puzzle into place. It would take another year, however, before the dream came to pass.

I was invited to attend a leadership conference our church was hosting a few weeks later. To my surprise, Pastor Steve Fatow was one of the guest speakers, as was my pastor. They shared the platform that morning and were both greatly used by God. My dear friend, Pastor Javier Espinoza, invited me to sit up front with all the pastors and special guests; afterwards he introduced me to some of them. One man I met was Pastor Josué Munoz, who was Pastor Steve's translator in Latin America. I felt blessed to shake hands with this great minister of the Gospel, as he and his father have been great pioneers in bringing the Gospel to remote regions in Guatemala and many other Latin American nations. Pastor Josué was also the president of "Prince of Peace International Ministries." After we chatted for a few minutes, he asked me if I would like to visit Guatemala. "Of course," I said, unable to contain the huge smile spreading across my face. That same day, Pastor Javier invited me to ride with them to the other city where Pastor Steve would be preaching at a crusade. My mother let me go, and, in spite of not having any spare clothes with me, God provided everything for me on the way. It was one of those days of divine favor, when many doors seemed to open at once. I was also overjoyed when Pastor Steve set the date for me to preach in his church in Knoxville the following year. The right time to make official plans had finally come.

A few months went by and one day the phone rang. It was the secretary of "Prince of Peace Church" in Guatemala. A date was booked, and a few days later we received an email with two plane tickets attached. I was very excited, since it had been almost three years since I had flown on a plane. That trip would become a pivotal one in my life, and God opened many doors for us there to minister in other Latin American nations. Over the course of a year, I returned to Guatemala several times. To God's glory, we held crusades in gyms, fields and even stadiums. It was an awesome stage in my life. I was privileged to witness to thousands of people at that time and each trip brought with it a precious new chapter, written by God's own hand. Guatemala had by now become the launching pad for our growing ministry. There, God was preparing my heart for the next level, giving me more opportunities to go through an intensive training on walking in the supernatural. It was a completely different ministerial terrain for us. We faced many challenges, yet also saw many miracles. It was a time when my heart grew closer to God and I learned to trust Him in everything, even in the face of danger.

"I was going to kill him."

My dad laughed nervously, thinking the man was joking. Marcos (we shall call him), turned and repeated the phrase again, this time looking directly at me. By the time he finished telling his incredible testimony, however, we realized that he was in fact serious.

Marcos had been a man utterly possessed by the enemy. He was in such bondage that the demons would torment him, urging him to commit terrible acts. The torture had started many years ago, after his wife passed away. He told us of how he had been flicking through the TV channels one day and come across an interview with me on TBN Enlace. As he was watching the program, the enemy spoke to Marcos, commanding him to bring me into town and kill me. "This demon actually gave me the whole plot," he told us, "I was to host you, and while you were preaching, I was supposed to kill you in exchange for my freedom."

The enemy had planted a seed of wickedness in this man's mind and Marcos had been determined to carry out the whole horrible scheme. He made all the necessary arrangements, inviting me to come and preach and even offering to host me. Amazingly, Marcos' "condition" had gone unnoticed by those around him and he still attended church. He was even in ministry, playing drums for the worship team and acting as a coordinator for events. At this point, I committed a mistake that could have cost me dearly – indeed, it nearly cost me my life.

Marcos had managed to mask his true state so well that I thought nothing of accepting his invitation. I had been so excited by the numerous opportunities to minister that I neglected to ask God if he was in it. I did, however, notice something odd when I was ministering one evening. The worship time was over, but Marcos stayed seated at the drum kit during the entire service, even while I was preaching. He explained how, during the ministration time, he had been ready to stab me – right there and then on the platform. Then something supernatural happened. Each time he reached into his back pocket for the knife, he felt an invisible hand grab him tightly around the wrist, stopping him from bringing it out. After trying several times to reach for the knife, without success, Marcos eventually gave up.

The following morning, I approached Marcos and asked, "Do you know of a place where we could go to pray? The house where we were staying is a little hectic." He offered to take my dad and me to his own home and said, "We will be able to pray there in peace." His house was located up in the hills, a good 45-minute drive from the town. Getting there seemed to take forever; not a whole lot of conversation took place in the car. When we finally arrived and walked into the house, my dad and I noticed something bizarre right away. The house was almost completely bare, except for a few pictures hanging on the wall. What little furniture Marcos had was covered in dust and looked strangely unused. The entire house looked so abandoned that we thought he must have taken us to a different place. We never imagined that someone actually occupied this derelict building. My dad and I fell into the trap of following Marcos into his room and received the fright of our lives when he began to manifest. In an instant, our prayer time unexpectedly became an intense battle.

I had very limited knowledge of spiritual warfare at the time and my dad had virtually none. We were shocked by the experience but recovered our wits enough to begin rebuking the demon. After doing so for a few minutes, we began to pray in tongues and Marcos fell backwards and collapsed. For the next hour, we prayed intensely that he would be set free from all demonic oppression. At some point, Marcos seemed to come back to his senses and my dad gave him a hand, helping him up. Then, as though nothing had happened, Marcos got into the car and drove us back.

God must have protected us on that trip back, because what we didn't realize was that Marcos was not yet completely free. The church intercessors were made aware of his situation and we were later told that it took three days of intense warfare to secure Marcos' total deliverance. Incredibly, Marcos eventually became an evangelist himself and started traveling in the local villages and towns, preaching the transforming power of our Lord Jesus Christ! Praise be to God!

Guatemala and Beyond

As our trips to Guatemala were became more frequent and, as the Lord opened doors in various cities across the nation, we saw more and more favor everywhere we went. Guatemala is a nation known for her past revivals and for being the most Christian country in all of Central America. It is home to some of the largest churches and more than half of the population have heard the Gospel and attend a Christian church. From the capital city to the high mountains of Peten, "home of the majestic Mayan pyramids," and from the Coasts of Port of San José to the borders of El Salvador, everywhere we went we saw God moving and a revival break out.

Since we were doing a lot of ministry inland, we often needed places to stay overnight for a few days. One person who graciously opened his home to us was a secular events coordinator. He was used to convening large events for famous bands and singers. He was a very well liked man and competent in all that he managed (including the crusade we were ministering at), but unfortunately he lacked character. Later on that trip, we discovered some very disturbing dealings that had been going on. We were very hurt to learn that this man had been taking advantage of us, asking various people for large sums of money to cover our airline tickets.

The city mayors and the local businessmen who were advertising their companies on posters and fliers at the crusade had already covered most of the expenses. The airline tickets, however, provided an opportunity for the man to make some money. Many pastors sensed that there was something wrong with this man, but it wasn't until everything came to light that they understood why they had been feeling that way. God gave my dad the wisdom he needed to confront the coordinator, but instead of repenting and correcting his behavior, he committed another terrible error. It was discovered that he was having an affair with one of the ladies in the crusade choir. That was the icing on the cake. This man was obviously bad news, and we had to stop working with him straight away.

During our trips to Guatemala, God molded, trained and disciplined us, giving us a crash course in crusade evangelism. The crusades were phenomenal, and in each town we visited, hundreds of souls came to Jesus and people were healed. There were powerful testimonies, from paralyzed children walking to people with unimaginable sorts of diseases being instantly healed.

We visited a small town on the outskirts of Escuintla (a city two hours from the capital), and were invited to go and pray for someone rather influential among the locals. When we came into this lady's home and prayed for her, we never expected other people to show up. But when she was healed and the word spread, more and more people came and crammed into her little house, also wanting prayer.

Many other beautiful healings took place there that day – it was as though the house was under a cloud of glory. I was reminded of the times when Jesus walked into the villages and healed people in their homes. Of course, even 2000 years later it was still Jesus who visited the house that day in Guatemala, healing the sick. From the early hours of the morning to late in the afternoon, dozens of families came by having heard what Jesus was doing in their street. We later heard that what took place made such an impact that it was never forgotten, becoming part of the town's history.

Rural Revivals

Sometimes, God led us to minister even in the most unusual places and situations. I was invited to share the Gospel in some surprising places. From Rotary Club meetings to Full Gospel Businessmen gatherings, prayer meetings at the National Army Training Academy to the Police Headquarters, and Women's Aglow meetings to private devotionals with diplomats – I had never before in my life been exposed to so many different settings in which to preach the Gospel. During one of those meetings, I met a lady, Ana Arriaza, whom God used very strategically to replace my previous coordinator. Ana was a very godly woman whom God used mightily to help us with our ministry.

One day, Ana asked me to pray for one of her uncle's factories. We drove to the factory to meet him and he gave us a tour of the premises. He took us into his office afterwards and asked us to pray for his staff. He was very touched by the Holy Spirit and begged us to visit his brother, Miguel, who lived in the hills of an area known as "Carretera al Salvador" (Road to The Savior), one of the wealthiest residential areas in Guatemala. Ana contacted her other uncle and he agreed to the proposal, saying that he would be happy to receive us.

So that same afternoon, we headed to Miguel's office and prayed over his staff. After we had finished, he invited us over for dinner the following day and asked if we would also pray for his family. We accepted his invitation and the next day, we started out for his home. We drove for about an hour and headed towards an even hillier area of the city. I didn't have a clue where we were going, and the narrow, paved road seemed to go on forever. It was also quite foggy and the weather conditions were not the best. After going up an impossibly steep road in the final ten minutes of the trip, we finally arrived.

Being at the mansion was an amazing experience – especially for a simple fifteen-year-old like me who had never seen one before. Not in real-life anyway – only in the movies had I seen such a grand house. The view was spectacular and the house was the biggest I had ever been in. When my dad and I walked into this "palace" we weren't really sure what to do, but after we started talking with the family the Holy Spirit took over. That same night, Miguel made a confession of faith and accepted Jesus as his personal savior. He didn't stop there, however, soon Miguel was on the phone, inviting all his friends to come to his house. Not wanting to waste any opportunity, he asked if we could pray for them so that they too could become Christians and be filled with the Holy Spirit!

Most of Miguel's friends who showed up that night had never been exposed to the Holy Spirit and were either Catholics or agnostics. What a glorious experience it was to minister to those precious people who all lived within a few blocks of each other.

There were many other impromptu revival meetings that came about spontaneously and many healings which took place not at large crusades, but rather at those small gatherings. We stayed in touch with Miguel after that day, continuing to visit him from time to time. Each time we saw him, we marveled at the difference God had made in his life. Miguel had his own helicopter and private helipad in his garden. He owned several banana farms all along the coast and was involved in several other business ventures. His life had been empty, until that day when the power of the Holy Spirit turned him upside down. Miguel developed a deep thirst for the Word of God and would spend many hours reading the Scriptures. He loved to discuss the Word with us, and in this way his house became something of a regular port of call for us when we were in Guatemala. On one occasion, Miguel even gave us a ride in his helicopter. It was used for a new purpose – evangelism! He had been talking to some of the pastors in the surrounding towns and had organized for them to rally together, even putting together a short evangelistic tour of the region. When we arrived, we were astonished to see stages and chairs set-up and worship teams ready for the meetings in the evening. It was amazing to see the body of Christ coming together in such unity. Many farmers in the area, who were impressed to see their boss facilitating such an event, came along and were touched by the power of God. Many of them were convicted of their sins and came to know Jesus Christ as their Savior. At each event, we saw the power of God at work, and revival broke out. There were also many reports of miraculous healings.

This kind of itinerant work became the norm in our ministry, and we went on to do more community outreaches – not only in Guatemala, but also in Mexico, Colombia and Nicaragua. With so many people being healed, saved and set free, however, the enemy wasn't taking it all lying down. Obviously unhappy that he was losing some of his V.I.Ps (witchdoctors, gang leaders, drug lords and the like), he fought back. As a result, we often found ourselves locked in an intense battle against evil. Such an incident occurred when we were invited to minister in one of the most dangerous towns in Nicaragua, one renowned for its gang activity. It was so bad, that even the local evangelist told us he feared going into town. There had been many horrible reports circulating about how preachers had been treated by gang members and the town actually became known as the place where "pastors are hung by their ties."

When we arrived, the place looked just as unsafe as we imagined it. It was obvious from the atmosphere of vandalism and crime that the local gang lords ruled the area. We held a healing crusade that evening on a dirt soccer field. On that first night, various churches from other towns came together. The place was packed and more than 500 people had come seeking God for a miracle.

At the end of the first night, we noticed that there was a small group of intimidating looking young men standing out on the soccer field, just to the left of the platform. What we didn't know was that they were actually members of one of the most feared gangs in town. My mom was with me on this trip, and when she saw them, she felt prompted in her spirit to approach them. The local pastors told us afterwards that no one had ever dared to witness to them, let alone a tall white woman from Costa Rica. As I prayed for the people that had responded to the altar call, out of the corner of my eye I saw my mom talking with the young men. I was seriously concerned about her welfare to be honest, but I decided to trust God. After the altar call, some of the men left but others lingered longer. When I talked to Mom about it later that night, she told me that some of them had actually promised to come back the following evening. To our absolute shock, not only did all of them show up, but they also made a commitment to Jesus Christ! Glory to God!

Open-air meetings often brought their own set of challenges, and there were times when we had to deal with the weather, technical issues, or a whole myriad of other problems. When it rained one night, the dirt floor we were standing on became a mud pit. Another night the power went out during the ministration time. We were concerned, thinking that the people were going to leave, but to our surprise, they not only stayed, but prayed all the more loudly! It seemed that every time something went wrong, God took advantage of those situations and used them for His glory.

One of the most powerful crusades I can remember happened in Colombia, where almost twenty thousand people showed up. It took place in Girardot, a small city two hours from Bogota City – a place known as "The Inferno" because of the record high temperatures they experienced each summer. When God hit it, "The Inferno" became an oasis of refreshment, flowing with the sweet breeze of His presence. Revival hit the entire city, and more than 3,000 people came to Christ during the whole crusade! The media became involved and suddenly the local TV networks wanted to film what God was doing. Crippled people began to walk, blind men recovered their sight, the deaf heard again and many were healed of tumors, hernias and all kinds of diseases. So many people were being healed that the doctors we had with us to verify the healings weren't able to keep up! It was an amazing and unforgettable crusade where God increased my faith and took me to a higher level.

Chapter 19

New Territory

After traveling extensively, speaking at crusades and conferences wherever the Lord led, we knew that something big was approaching. There was the sense we were entering a new season in the ministry. This was confirmed when we received an invitation to attend a parliamentary session in Costa Rica and share for a few minutes during recess. My friend, Senator Justo Orozco, had asked that I share briefly with the other senators what the Lord had done in my life. Although I was quite nervous, when I finished speaking I was amazed to see that the glass on the table next to me remained untouched. God had settled my nerves and given me the grace I needed! Throughout my childhood it had been prophesied on many occasions that I would stand before dignitaries and testify of God's goodness, but I never dreamt it would happen so soon!

Afterwards, Senator Orazco took me into his office and asked me to pray for his staff and his political party's volunteers. As we prayed, I felt God's presence fill the room, and I knew that

He was at work in the hearts of the people. The meeting became a precious time of worship and prayer. When it was over, Mr. Orazco asked me if there was anything he could do for me. I told him of the invitation I had received to minister in one of the churches in Tennessee, asking him if he could write a support letter to help me obtain my very first United States visa. Within a couple of days, he had not only arranged the support letter, but had also personally contacted the United States Embassy, asking that my visa be considered favorably.

The following week, I found myself standing before a large, beige colored building – The United States Embassy. When the doors were opened and we passed through security, I felt a sense of awe and trepidation. I had never before been inside the building nicknamed, "The House of Frights." It had earned that name by the many applicants who had been denied a visa on account of missing documentation. As we made the line, we began to pray – hard. My heart pounded inside my chest. I never imagined I would feel so much anxiety in an embassy – I had, after all, been through the process of getting visas for other countries many times before. As I stood there with my parents, waiting for my turn, I noticed that there was a mean looking guy assigned to the interview window at the front of my line. I began to pray, "Lord, please may we not talk to this guy but to the nice lady next to him."

God intervened supernaturally, and we were asked to wait in the other line. After what seemed an eternity, we reached the front and the lady took our paperwork. To me, the sound of her flicking through the documents was deafening. Seeing the microphones built into the windows, I dared not even speak. The immigration officer asked us three simple questions, smiled, and stamped our applications. "You have been approved and your passports will be ready this afternoon for you to pickup. Enjoy your stay in the United States." When we heard these words, our hearts leapt for joy! I think I must have said, "Thank you," about four times as I left the window! We enjoyed a wonderful ride home that afternoon, rejoicing and praising the Lord the whole way.

A month later, we were airborne and on our way to the United States of America. God supernaturally provided us with three plane tickets and enough funds to pay for airport taxes, food and other necessities. Once again, we saw Him taking care of all our travel arrangements and making a way. When family members and friends heard about our trip, they greatly blessed us with offerings and donations.

On October 23, 2003, around 4:30 p.m., the pilot finally said over the intercom, "Ladies and Gentlemen, in a few minutes we will begin our descent into Dallas International Airport." Although we would only be in Dallas, Texas for a few hours, when I heard those words, I quickly pulled up my window shade to have a look at the city of my dreams.

I say "the city of my dreams" because God had already been speaking to me for many years about Dallas. As a youngster, I loved to watch the "Texas Ranger" series, and dreamt of one day visiting the beautiful city it was set in. I had even received prophetic words that in the future I would move to Dallas.

The first dream was about to come to pass, and unknown

to me, the second part would be fulfilled in a few years time. For the moment though, I was content to look out my airplane window, pondering the dawn of a new season.

Chapter 20

Chasing After The Double Portion

At this point, I would like to share with you another key principle God has used in the past to guide me towards His destiny. It is the idea of chasing after the double portion. Early on in my ministry, God taught me that dissatisfaction is actually my ally. He taught me to always dream for more, and that once one dream was fulfilled, a greater one would be given in its place. Remember though, dear friend, that "impossible" dreams are to glorify God, and have very little to do with our own efforts or capabilities. In fact, often God realizes dreams in our lives *in spite of* our capabilities.

God wants us to be radical for Him. We are radical when we are not satisfied with what we see; when we bring positive change to our environment rather than being content with things the way they are. We are radical when we are willing to push forward, no matter what obstacles we face along the way. The prophet Elisha was someone who knew what it was to be radical. He was willing to go whatever distance it took to receive a double portion of his master Elijah's spirit. In the book of Kings we read the account;

> Elijah took his coat, rolled it up and struck the [River Jordan] with it. The water was divided to the right and to the left, and the two of them crossed over on dry ground. When they had crossed, Elijah said to Elisha, "Tell me what I can do for you before I am taken from you." "Let me inherit a double portion of your spirit," Elisha replied. 2 Kings 2: 1-11 (NIV)

What spirit did Elisha speak of? It was none other than *The* Spirit of God dwelling in Elijah, the precious Ruach Ha'Kadosh, or Holy Spirit. This is the secret of living a radical life and fulfilling the dreams God has given us – to be filled with His Holy Spirit. We live in a society which is desperately thirsty for the supernatural. Often though, people go looking in the wrong places – going to see psychics, by looking to the "New Age," watching supernaturally themed movies and dabbling in the occult. I believe that one of the reasons people seek after these things is because of the spiritual vacuum that exists (particularly in Western societies). It is a void that has been created by the absence of God's supernatural power in the lives of many believers today. If you and I truly walked in the power of God's Spirit, we would see communities and even whole societies transformed.

When we decide to live radical lives, we should not be

surprised if the enemy rises up against us. He is not intimidated in the least by a Christian who attends church once a week and maintains a normal, comfortable life. When the people of God begin to understand His calling and purpose for their lives however, and begin to walk in His will, they suddenly become a threat. It is then that opposition arises and the battle begins for all those wanting to make a difference.

So where do we start? When Elisha received his calling (1 Kings 19:19) he was plowing oxen. This indicates that Elisha was simply going about his daily duties at the time. He was obviously a diligent and hard worker. While we wait for God to call us, we must "plough" our hearts by dedicating ourselves to studying the Word and spending time with the Lord. In this way, we ensure that the soil of our hearts is fertile, ready to receive the dream-seeds God wants to plant within us. When we have been faithful, we must also be willing to step out when the time is right.

There was an obstacle that Elisha had to overcome at this point. Would he cling to the familiar comfort of his everyday life, and to all that he had known, or would he step out and respond to the Lord's calling? When Elijah called Elisha, he did not hesitate. In a flash, Elisha had packed up, kissed his mom and dad goodbye and was off!

For him to take such a drastic step, something profound must have happened in his heart. The Word gives us a clue,

"So Elijah went from there and found Elisha son of Shaphat. He was plowing with twelve yoke of oxen, and he himself was driving the twelfth pair. Elijah went up to him and threw his cloak around him. Elisha then left his oxen and ran after Elijah…" 1 Kings 19:19 (NIV)

Elisha had an encounter with the supernatural.

There was transference of the Spirit of God onto Elisha, when Elijah's anointing–saturated mantle was thrown over him. In the Bible, a mantle can also represent *authority*. When Elisha received his calling, he was also equipped with the authority he needed to see the task through. For this very reason, we can embrace our own callings without fear. Fear is a weapon of the enemy designed to hold us back, but God promises that he has already given us the authority we need to overcome any obstacles brought against us,

> "I have given you authority to trample on snakes and scorpions and to overcome all the power of the enemy; nothing will harm you." Luke 10:19 (NIV)

Two obstacles that Elisha faced on the day of Elijah's ascension to heaven were intimidation and discouragement. When his fellow prophets tried to stop him from continuing on with Elijah, Elisha refused to give up on his dream. He was determined to ask Elijah for the double portion.

Elisha continued on, almost aggressive in the pursuit of his destiny. So must we also be if we want to see God do great things with our lives. We too must be active in seeking more of God's anointing and power. We cannot expect to receive a significant spiritual blessing from God without being committed to relentlessly seeking His face. All spiritual blessings are rooted in and grow out of cultivating a deep intimacy with God.

Each of the places Elisha visited in his journey with Elijah represents a prophetic season in his destiny. First, Elisha left *Gilgal* and followed Elijah to *Bethel*. *Gilgal* represents the beginning of Elisha's spiritual journey. Gilgal literally means, "Rolling," referring to God having "rolled away the reproach of Egypt" from His people (Joshua 5:9). It was also the site where all the Israelite males where circumcised who were born in the desert and had not yet been consecrated to God. In our own spiritual journey, Gilgal represents the moment when we are set apart for God, when He cleanses us and sets us free from the reproach of our past. It is also when we enter into a covenant with God by the shedding of Jesus' blood on the cross; when we commit to belong to Him and surrender our lives to his service.

The Hebrew meaning of the word Bethel is "House of God" or, "Gate of Heaven." It was there that Jacob had a vision of a ladder going into heaven, his first powerful God-encounter. For us, this speaks of the vital importance of having a life-changing encounter with our Creator. It is at our own "Bethel" that God shapes and molds our character with His presence. There our lives are transformed by His power and our communion with Him is taken to another level.

Elisha left Bethel and continued on to Jericho, the historic place of Israel's victory. In order to take the city, the people of God walked around its walls seven times. These walls were supposedly unmovable and indestructible; the pride of the city, but God tore them down in a matter of seconds. This was made possible when a courageous people who had lived through God's process dared to believe Him for a miracle. It is time for you to inherit what God has promised you. It is time to enter your Jericho and tear down the walls that have been preventing you from entering the Promised Land.

Finally, the last destination Elisha reached was the River Jordan. The Jordan is the place where we receive the fulfillment of God's promises and see them come to pass. It is the supernatural place where we walk in our destiny. Just as Elisha and Elijah parted the waters of the Jordan using their mantle, the only way for you to walk across your Jordan is using the mantle of the anointing God has given you. As you flow in His anointing, you will see the miraculous and walk in the fullness of your calling.

From Music City to the Sunshine State

The day finally came when my mom, my dad and I landed in Nashville, Tennessee. When my Aunt Maria saw us standing there at the airport with our suitcases in hand, she ran and hugged us. There was a lot of emotion that day, and even some tears shed, as we all talked of how God made it possible for us to be there.

God opened many doors while we were in Nashville and Knoxville. Not only was I able to realize the long time dream of preaching in Pastor Steve Fatow's church, Trinity Chapel, but suddenly, I also found myself preaching on TV and radio, as well as in other churches. God was being glorified all the time! When our time in Tennessee came to an end, we felt very sad, but were also convinced that one day we would be back – God surely had more in store for the future.

My Aunt had also been very impacted by the turn of events while we were Nashville. She had never heard me preach and came out to one of our evening services. She was astounded by the move of God's power, and ever since that night, she caught the dream of reaching the nations with the Gospel. An exceptional woman, with a strong work ethic and infectious personality, my Aunt Maria would later become an integral part of the ministry.

For our next visit to Nashville, we came with yearlong visas, unsure of how long we would be in the United States. All we knew was that we were available for whatever the Lord wanted to grant us. God faithfully opened doors in many new churches, and before we knew it, we were traveling and ministering in other states. I received an invitation to visit Little Rock, Arkansas, for an outreach program. After ten hours of driving, we finally arrived. Maria was driving, and every time she was behind the wheel it was an adventure!

By now, Maria had thoroughly caught the vision and she began to coordinate for us. A few media outlets became aware of my story, and to our surprise, suddenly I was being asked to attend interviews for channels seven, five and two. Some journalists also published the testimony of my healing in their papers. What surprised us most of all, however, was that during this season no one persecuted us. The media actually seemed to have a genuine interest in what God was doing.

One day, an invitation came from a Romanian lady, asking us to minister at her church in Davie, Florida. She had spoken to her pastor, who initially wanted us to come for three nights of meetings. What we could not predict was that revival would break out in the church and the meetings would be extended for four more days. They became the first weeklong meetings in the history of our ministry. Miracles, healings and signs took place and suddenly the local media were there, covering the meetings. Through this experience, we were reminded once again that in God there truly are no limits; and that as His people we should never, ever underestimate what He can do. His power is limitless, and He will do as He pleases.

It was an incredible time under the presence of God. My short stay in Davie prepared me for the other meetings we still had upcoming.

We travelled south to Miami, Florida where I visited with a pastor friend of Pastor Javier's. I had been introduced to him once before, in Costa Rica. He prayed for me in his office and felt in his spirit to support our ministry. He extended an invitation and asked me if I could preach at his church on Thursday night. "Alpha and Omega" is one of the largest churches in Miami, so it was an amazing privilege to be asked to preach. That night, the Holy Spirit moved in a very special way. Little did I know, "Alpha and Omega" would actually become my home church when I moved to Miami, a couple of years later.

After that awesome visit to Miami, we packed our bags and headed to the airport. It was time to go home. While we were waiting to board our flight, we received a phone call from the producer of one of the top TV shows in Latin America, "Don Francisco Presenta." We were stunned! Don Francisco had been working in television for over thirty years and was a household name among Hispanics. We could never have dreamt of such an incredible opportunity to share the Gospel!

Sadly though, when they asked if we could stay on in Miami for longer, we realized that it was too late to change our plans. We flew home with a strong sense of disappointment.

Two days after we arrived back, however, we were surprised with another phone call. The producer again asked me to appear on the show, and informed us that all of our expenses would be paid for, including airfare and hotel accommodations for a week. We were astonished by the offer, but still decided to pray about it. I had learned my lesson from the incident in Guatemala when Marcos wanted to kill me! God gave us the green light, and before we knew it, we were on our way back to Miami, much, much sooner than we had ever expected!

When we arrived, we were taken to the hotel to rest. A few hours later, we were picked up and driven to the station. I was given a few minutes to speak with Don Francisco before the show and discovered he was very different from the guy I was used to seeing on television. He was very open and friendly, and even asked me questions about the Lord.

During our chat, he told me that he had been brought up in a Jewish family in Chile. In the interview he was very supportive of the calling God had put on my life, even asking me to stand in front of the studio audience and preach as though I were in a stadium. I began to do so, when suddenly it struck me – the audience I was preaching to was, in fact, far larger than any I could ever reach in a stadium. The people seated in front of me were only a fraction of those who would be watching the program. Most of the viewers were invisible to me, those thousands who would be sitting in their homes listening to the Gospel. God alone gave me the strength I needed that night to honor perhaps the greatest opportunity I have ever had to speak his Word.

After that, we ministered from California to New York and just about everywhere in between. Wherever we were invited and the Lord permitted, we preached the good news of the Gospel, even in city hall meetings. God also used this pivotal time in my life to launch us into worldwide ministry. Soon we were holding crusades in the Caribbean, as well as South America.

My dad and I continued to travel together, ministering and seeing God's glory. I thank God so much for my parents – He gave me the best travel companion I could ever hope for in my dad. Mom and Dad made so many sacrifices to facilitate the ministry's expansion, even being apart from each other from time to time. Nevertheless, every time there was an opportunity, they made the effort for us to travel together or alternated between themselves, traveling back and forth to care for my other siblings.

Chapter 21

Worldwide Evangelism

For a while, I had been dealing with the lingering thought of how awesome it would be to preach the Gospel to other cultures. I desired Alejandro Arias International Ministries to be a truly multicultural ministry and my dream was to bring as many people as possible to Jesus Christ!

Pastor Steve Fatow and I had become good friends by this time, and he invited me back his church in Knoxville. Something that really touched my heart one night was seeing even the little kids on the floor, under the power of God. All of them were crying, longing for more of the Holy Spirit. After the service, I was approached by an older Filipino lady who asked me if I had ever wanted to go to the Philippines. Trying to hide my excitement, I responded carefully, "Yes, I would love to one day."

That evening, we all went to dine at a beautiful Asian restaurant. During the meal, the lady, whose name was Nimfa, and my evangelist friend, Patty, began to plan a trip to the Philippines.

A few months later, on August 20, 2004, we embarked on a journey that would take us to the other side of the world. Making the journey with me were our friends from the United States, Patty Clemens and Elizabeth Crown, my Aunt Maria, Sister Nimfa, and my dad. When we arrived in Los Angeles after a five-hour flight, I was feeling great – what I did not realize, however, was that we were only about a quarter of the way to our destination. I had no idea how long the flight would be from Los Angeles to Manila in the Philippines, all the way across the Pacific Ocean. When I found out the duration of our flight from an attendant, I just about passed out!

After a long fifteen hours in the sky, we touched down in Manila, two days after our departure. It was then that I had my first true taste of jet lag. Having crossed the International Date Line, it was pretty harsh. It hit us all so hard we could barely function during the first couple of days of our tour. It would be a few years before I would learn how to manage jet lag, although, sometimes it is near impossible. We took a short flight from Manila down to Davao, "The Muslim capital of Philippines." When we arrived, we were amazed and touched to see a whole delegation of people waiting for us at the airport with welcome signs and gifts. We were taken to the houses we would be staying in, and later that evening we attended a Pastors' dinner.

There were about a hundred pastors at the dinner, and we enjoyed a wonderful time of fellowship over the delicious food. After we ate, Nimfa approached me and asked me to preach. I wondered how I could, because back then my English was not very good. As I wrestled with the idea, they called my name, and there I was, standing in front of a hundred pastors. I used one of the only words I knew in English about fifty times- "Revival!" That was just about all my message was about, and since I was so exhausted by the trip, I had forgotten all the sermons I had planned on preaching. With help from my Aunt, and above all, with the help of the Holy Spirit (who came to my rescue!), the service turned out to be powerful. After the meeting, all the pastors came forward and received prayer.

For two weeks, we saw God moving and revival breaking out in various communities. God's power was not limited to move in churches alone. We experienced His glory even in public school soccer fields, with more than eight hundred kids gathered to hear the Gospel. I remember one of those meetings well, which took place in a private Catholic high school. There was a sea of children of all ages sitting in front of the stage, all wearing their blue uniforms. When I was given the microphone, I was amazed at how respectful and quiet they were during the message and how responsive they were to the Gospel. While I was still preaching, the power suddenly went out and the microphone stopped working. The children giggled, and I felt lost for a moment. What would I do now?

Thankfully, one of the teachers handed me a mega-phone and I was able to continue with the message. This reminded me of the early days, preaching in the park in Alajuela, and I felt that same passion I felt back in Costa Rica. We were blessed to see hundreds of hands raised that day, in response to the Gospel, as children said the salvation prayer and came to Jesus Christ! Over the next week, we were taken to every place you could imagine:

universities, high schools, government offices and churches, all across the big city of Davao. We prayed for many hungry people who were desperate to hear the good news of the Gospel. Our time in the Philippines was truly unforgettable, and it would come to mark the beginning of a greater international scope in the ministry.

Chapter 22

Kingdom Culture

Ironically, just as the ministry was beginning to take on a more multicultural focus, God began to teach me about quite another concept altogether – "Kingdom Culture." We belong to a powerful Kingdom and have the privilege of enjoying intimate fellowship with its ruler, Christ the King. Yet, there is also one other essential element. We are called to be co-workers with Christ. This means that we not only have the privilege of being part of His Kingdom, but we also have the honor of working as part of one body in Christ for his Kingdom's advancement. We are to participate in the Kingdom's advancement by using every resource available to us to take the message to the four corners the globe. However, we can't be part of something unless we know how it functions, and in order to understand how the Kingdom works and be part of it, we must know the Kingdom's culture.

Culture is something that has always fascinated me. I enjoy learning about different world cultures, the collection of customs, foods, habits, dress, ways of thinking, traditions etc. that give people a sense of belonging and is often tied to their nationality. Each country has its own traits. For instance, in my home country of Costa Rica, many of us love the famous national dish, "Gallo Pinto," for breakfast each morning. This is a dish consisting of rice and beans mixed together. It is an important part of our culture.

Just as Costa Rica and all countries have their own foods and identifying characteristics, so the Kingdom of God also has a specific culture. The citizens of His Kingdom should be known by being part of this culture. In a way, this means that we are dual citizens – first of the Kingdom of God, and secondly of our own earthly nations. If there is any question about how we should live, we should look first and foremost at how the Word (our Kingdom Manual) instructs us to live. In this way, we will be able to begin building God's Kingdom on earth and influencing the societies we live in. Sadly though, there is often reluctance among many believers to fully embrace their new identity and culture. In order to live Kingdom Culture, we need to know the character of "The King." Everything in God's Kingdom is a reflection of His very person. If we love Him and know Him, we will know His likes, dislikes, sorrows, hopes and the dreams of His heart. These should set the pattern for our footsteps.

In order to walk as a Kingdom citizen, it is also important that we have the correct perception of our King. Religion encourages us to see God as angry, punishing and distant, rather than as a deeply caring, tender and compassionate Father. Or, there is the reverse – seeing God as so gracious and loving that

He is incapable of justly punishing wrong doing. Each view is equally unbalanced. God is a loving God, but He is also awesomely holy and absolutely just. If we embrace all attributes of God's character, these can actually help us love Him more. For example, knowing the extent of God's love for us as sinners *in spite of* His infinite power and Holiness can leave us even more in awe of His person.

Once we begin to truly know God, all aspects of Kingdom Culture, such as prayer, fasting, worship, tithing and warfare become a delight to us, rather than a burden. As we begin to live according to the original spiritual pattern that we were created to live by, we will know a greater level of purpose and satisfaction. As we live thus, we will be changed to our very core, and our relationship with God will consistently grow and flourish.

What so many of us have failed to see for a long time is that a religious, traditional, dogmatic prayer life cannot keep the fire alive in our relationship with Him. When praying has become common to you, watch out! You could be losing your first love. Remember that when you see prayer as a sacrifice, rather than as an offering you delight to bring, it will be twice as hard for your flesh to submit to doing it. Prayer is meant to be the gift of direct communication with God, a privilege for His children to enjoy.

As the psalmist David wrote,

"Better is one day in your courts than a thousand elsewhere." Psalm 84:10 (NIV)

A Kingdom Generation

As friends of God and citizens of His Kingdom, it is vital that we as the church learn about our identity as Kingdom people. In order for the church to advance, we must have a Kingdom mentality. The importance of the Kingdom was very much emphasized by Jesus during His earthly ministry. He spoke about the Kingdom in most of his parables. In fact, Jesus referred to The Kingdom around one hundred and five times in the Gospels. This would indicate that He believed it was relevant and important for Him to leave a Kingdom Culture established among His own disciples. As we transition from the traditional church model to a Kingdom one, even our way of thinking must change. We are no longer to be bound to a religious lifestyle, but rather we are to be committed to pursuing an intimate and personal relationship with the King of Kings. Only out of that deep relationship can we know who we are in Christ – we are royalty.   The church must realize that Jesus wants to restore our true identity as the princes and princesses of God.

It should be noted here, that when we talk in terms of princes and princesses, we are not referring to fantasy figures, like those we might find in a children's movie, or titles that boost our self-esteem. Rather, we are referring to an army of royalty who know their true identity in Christ and are equipped in His power to stand against the tide of evil threatening to drown humanity.

If we experience the security which comes from knowing who we are in Christ, we will be ready to do great conquests in

His name. That is why the enemy is so intent upon destroying the identity of God's people and the church as a whole.

As Christians, we should be imitators of Christ. Therefore, the commission given to Christ in Isaiah also belongs to us, and provides us with guidelines for how we are to live:

"The Spirit of the Sovereign Lord is on me,
because the Lord has anointed me
to preach good news to the poor.
He has sent me to bind up the broken-hearted,
to proclaim freedom for the captives
and release from darkness for the prisoners,
to proclaim the year of the Lord's favor
and the day of vengeance of our God,
to comfort all who mourn."   Isaiah 61:1-4 (NIV)

Reading this passage, we see four vital aspects of Jesus' ministry. His mission was to preach the Gospel, heal the broken-hearted, set the captives free and prophesy (proclaim God's will). These should form the pillars of Kingdom Culture's impact on the world.

Another important aspect of our identity is that of being a co-heir with Christ. Being a co-heir not only means that we will share in Christ's eternal glory (Romans 8:17), but that we will also inherit the results of Isaiah 61's fulfillment.

In preaching the good news to the poor, we too can reap a mighty harvest of souls. When we pray for the sick and oppressed, we too have access to God's supernatural power manifested. God makes the mind of Christ known to us, so that we can proclaim His will to the world and help others have a relationship with Jesus,

> "…We have the mind of Christ."
> 1 Corinthians 2:16 (NIV)

We can also claim salvation, healing, freedom and communion with God for ourselves personally. We do not have to wait until heaven to experience Kingdom Culture. God has a new lifestyle for us to enjoy, right now, right here on earth.

Chapter 23

Favor

I was in Los Angeles, not to get on a big jumbo jet and fly somewhere else this time, but to attend a conference. It was April 25, 2006, and I had been invited by a pastor friend to attend a big conference commemorating the 100-year anniversary of the Azusa street revival. Standing there by the gate of the Los Angeles Convention Center, I was overwhelmed by the number of delegates I saw flowing in. Thousands of pastors and leaders had flown in from all over the world to be part of this historic event. As one body, we were going to celebrate one of the greatest revivals in our century, one that gave birth to many other revivals and worldwide moves of God. I felt like I was at a United Nations congress; the diversity of nationalities represented at the conference was astounding. On the second night, as I was standing in line to pay for my dinner, the lady next to me looked at my name tag and struck up a conversation. I found out that she was originally from Malaysia but was living in Australia. Although it seemed to be a chance meeting, I had the sense that God was arranging a divine connection. The lady's name was Vera Lim, and she invited me to sit at her table. She introduced me to her friends, many of whom were Indonesian pastors, and asked me to tell them my story. Although I had no idea at the time, God was using Vera to connect me with Bethany Church in Indonesia. I would preach there one day, and consequently many doors would be opened throughout South East Asia.

At the end of the third day, there was a session scheduled in the program, which I certainly didn't want to miss. Pastor Benny Hinn would be speaking. I had heard him preach in person once before in Guatemala, where he prayed for me. My friend Peter Plucick was there on that occasion, coordinating for Benny Hinn in Latin America. Peter took me aside, asking me if I would like to receive prayer at the close of the service. When I replied "Yes," Peter gave me a few instructions. He made a space for me in the front row and advised me to sit there and wait until he could come and get me. After the preaching was over and miracles began to happen, Pastor Hinn felt in his spirit to pray for a few pastors. Seizing the opportunity, Peter ran across the platform, grabbed me by the hand, and pulled me up onto the stage. It was quite an exhilarating moment! When he saw me standing there, Pastor Hinn called me forward. When he prayed for me, I literally felt as though I was imploding with the power of God. And he didn't pray just once; he prayed over me seven times! The seventh time, I was so overcome by the anointing that I couldn't get up off the floor; the ushers had to drag me off the platform and help me back to my seat. It was an overwhelming time under God's glory; an experience I had never forgotten.

The following day, I was scheduled to preach at a conference at "Prince of Peace," with my dear friend, Dr. Josué Munoz. Henry Hinn, Benny Hinn's brother, also happened to be preaching at one of the sessions. Afterwards, we all gathered in Dr. Josué's office, where I had the blessing of meeting Henry. I had tried to keep in touch with Pastor Henry since that day, but eventually we lost contact.

Now here I was, standing amongst thousands of believers in the Los Angeles Convention Center for the final night of the "Azusa Street Centennial Celebration." There was an atmosphere of expectation and the anointing was quite strong. As I worshipped God, I heard Him speak to my heart, asking, "Would you like to meet my servant, Benny Hinn?" "Of course, Lord. I would like that very much," I replied. Having already planned each step of the way, the Lord asked me to stay back after the meeting and wait to one side of the stage. After everything wrapped up, I headed over and waited. Eventually, the building was almost empty and it was getting quite late – they were already starting to turn off some of the lights. Pastor Benny Hinn and his staff had long left the platform, and all I could see were some security personnel around the back stage exits. I decided to take matters into my own hands for a moment and approached one of them, stating my petition. With a gruff "No," I was sent on my way. With no discernible way of seeing things come to pass, I prayed instead to the Lord, wondering how on earth it was all going to be possible.

Suddenly I heard the Holy Spirit say, "Stay here until I

show you what to do." After a few minutes, who should walk out from back stage but my new friend Vera Lim! She looked at me kindly, and asked what I was doing. After I explained the situation, she nodded and walked out. Five minutes later, Henry Hinn emerged from backstage and greeted me with a big smile and a hug. He then took me by the hand and led me straight to the green room. Suddenly, I found myself inside, standing in front of Pastor Benny Hinn. Pastor Henry interrupted the meeting in a loud voice and introduced me. It was all a little too quick for me to process, and all I could do was smile weakly and shake hands.

Pastor Benny prayed briefly for me and turned to Claudio Freidzon, asking if he had ever heard of "the boy preacher." Pastor Claudio nodded, said he had, and came around to give me a hug. That day, I so much felt the love of my Heavenly Daddy in a very tangible, real way. Moments later, Pastor Benny had to leave, and it was all over.

One Day of God's Favor...

God can indeed do extraordinary things in a single day. The event I have described illustrates this. This is also true of situations when God begins to accelerate processes you have been working through, perhaps for many years. I have heard it said, "One day of God's favor is worth seven years of labor," meaning, in a single day, God can bring to pass what you have been striving to achieve for years. It is all about timing.

When we learn to obey His commands and walk in His 'kairos' time, God will open doors for us we could never open ourselves and show us His favor. As the Scriptures remind us, it is,

"...Not by might nor by power, but by my Spirit,' says the LORD Almighty.'" Zechariah 4:6 (NIV)

The events at the "Azusa Street Centennial Celebration" marked the beginning of a new level in our ministry. More doors began to open internationally, and we received invitations from countries I had only dreamt of visiting. It was as though God had decided to quicken our steps.

Chapter 24

Boy Preacher To Man

After traveling with my dad for almost eight years, neither one of us could imagine what it would be like to travel alone. However, the time was fast approaching when the Lord would release my father from his years of faithful support. On the eve of my nineteenth birthday, both of my parents flew from Costa Rica to spend some time with me in Florida. By this time, I was now living in Miami, having recently relocated the ministry base to the United States. I went with my friend and fellow evangelist Luz Linares to pick up my parents at the airport. That weekend, we would be staying with her family and celebrating my birthday together. We waited for my parents to come out of the arrival gate…and waited…and waited. Two hours later, we sensed that something was very wrong. Another hour passed by and finally my mom emerged from the gate, looking very weary and sad. After we greeted one another, I anxiously asked where dad was.

Mom burst into tears, and began to tell us of the awful

events that had transpired.

They had been standing at the immigration booth, waiting for the officer to stamp their passports, brimming with excitement at seeing their son again after a few months of separation. After waiting a little while, they sensed that the officer was taking much longer than usual. The officer asked them a few questions about the purpose of their visit and listened silently to their replies, taking notes. Without any explanation, he turned, said something to the officer standing nearby and motioned for my parents to follow him. They were shown to a small interview room and were about to go inside, when the officer stopped my mom. "Just him," the officer said, jerking his thumb at my dad. By then very frightened, my mom went to sit down and wait on a small bench nearby. Finally an officer emerged and informed her that my father's visa had been cancelled and that he would be deported.

We were shocked to hear her story, and so terribly sad that my dad would not be able to be with us for my birthday. We were also grieved that he had to stay in a cell for the night, until his flight home could be changed. We discovered that the reason he was deported was because his visa belonged to the wrong sub-class. My father had been carrying a religious visa at the time, from his travels with me, and hadn't realized that he needed to apply for a tourist visa.

I was so disappointed and confused I could hardly pray that night. Why was this happening? Who would travel with me now? Would my father ever be able to visit the United States again? As these thoughts flashed through my mind, I felt worry and fear build up inside of me. Exhausted, I finally fell asleep. My mom and I discussed the possibility of making an appeal against the decision the following morning. We prayed together, but sensed that God wanted us to leave things as they were. He gave us His peace, and we tried to make the most of the rest of our time together.

Although it was an awful experience, I know today that God truly does cause "all things work together for good to those who love [Him], to those who are called according to *His* purpose." Romans 8:28 (NKJV) The Lord used the situation of my dad's deportation to help me step into manhood. It came to mark the beginning of a new season of personal growth and encouraged me to reply upon the Holy Spirit even more than before.

Coming into the Stature of the Perfect Man.

Growth is an absolutely necessary part of our lives. When the apostle Paul spoke of "coming into the stature of the perfect man," he was referring to the process that all of God's people experience constantly. It is the daily process of being alive in Christ and dying to the old man and the old nature.

> "You were taught, with regard to your former way of life, to put off your old self, which is being corrupted by its deceitful desires; to be made new in the attitude of your minds; and to put on the new self, created to be like God in true righteousness and holiness." Ephesians 4:22-24 (NIV)

Paul speaks of a progressive and transforming process in which the human character becomes the character of Christ. It is not an easy transition, and it requires the death of many parts of our human nature in order to allow the Lord Jesus Christ to live and reign in our hearts. This is how the Lord transforms our mentality and way of being, by placing His very person inside us. He molds us; just as the Potter forms a vessel. Reaching the stature of the perfect man means that we grow into the character of Christ.

Chapter 25

To The Ends Of The Earth

It was the third week of July, 2007. After fifteen months of intense prayer and perseverance, I was finally going to Australia. Rarely have I ever experienced so much opposition to a trip! It seemed that every way I turned, the enemy wanted to thwart God's plans. The very fact that I even arrived on Australian soil was a miracle in itself. The opportunity came about when Vera (who I became good friends with) arranged for me to travel to Perth, Western Australia. I would preach at Bethany Church, Perth (a daughter church of the much larger Bethany Church in Indonesia). After being given an invitation letter from the church, I submitted my visa application to the Australian Embassy in Washington and waited. Two weeks later, I received a letter in the mail informing me that my application had been refused. I stared at the letter in my hands for a moment, dumbfounded, before tearing it into pieces. "Devil, you are not winning this battle," I said under my breath. I had dealt with many visas in the past, but this one in particular had a lot of meaning for me. There was the sense that God was going to do something big on this trip – I had been looking forward to it ever since I met a delegation from Perth at the "Azusa Street Centennial Celebration." I knew very little about Perth, but had heard about what God was doing there from my mentor, Pastor Orlando Lopez. Orlando had gone to Perth the year before, where he stayed for almost three months, preaching and teaching in several churches. He was hosted by Francisco Rodriguez, a generous Salvadoran pastor who graciously provided him with everything he needed during the trip. Orlando spoke to Pastor Francisco about me, and when he returned to Costa Rica he put us both in touch. When I called Francisco for the first time, I told him of my impending trip in July and was excited when he suggested we put together an event. Over the next few months, he worked hard to coordinate a bilingual healing crusade. In the meantime, I was still struggling with visa issues. One thing is for certain – when great things are about to happen, even the enemy can sense it. He tries to do what he can to stop a mighty move of God, and that is why we face opposition. But, praise be to God – we have the victory!

Bearing this in mind, I decided to try another strategy. With time running out fast, it was time for drastic action. Some friends of mine had suggested that my application would be looked upon more favorably if I applied in person. There was one small catch – I could not re-apply at the same embassy, I would have to go to another one. The next closest Australian Embassy was in Mexico City. It seemed like the only course of action, so I hopped on the next available flight and headed south of the border.

I went early to the Embassy the next day and re-submitted my paperwork. After a couple of hours of waiting, however, I was told to go home, that the process would take longer. I could come back in three days and the visa should be ready. Three days passed and when I came back there was still no progress. "A technical issue with the computer system," I was told. After ten days of fasting, praying and waiting for a miracle, the breakthrough finally came and I was issued with my first ever Australian visa!

Two days later, on July 19, 2007, I was on my way to Perth, Australia. When I arrived, completely sleep-deprived, all I wanted to do was curl up in a corner and fall asleep. Because of the visa issues, my arrival coincided almost exactly with the start of the healing crusade. And so, it was straight from the airport to the venue. In spite of being so tired that I could barely find the passage I was going to preach on, when I got up to speak, I received a shot of strength from the Holy Spirit. He completely took over the service and moved mightily that evening. Two hours after arriving on Australian soil, I began to sense that God had a very unique purpose for me during this trip. What I never in my wildest dreams could have imagined was that, one day, I would call Australia home.

Chapter 26

An Unexpected Romance

After that first conference in Australia was over, I was led to the green room, where a meal had been prepared for all the pastors who attended the event. A tall young woman served me dinner, and I began to chat with those at the table. Yes, there it is in case you missed it. I had just met my future wife. And no one completely missed it more than me.

You see, I had one rule and one rule only – to ignore all girls and keep well away from them. I had made a decision from when I was very young to remain set apart for the Lord for my entire life. In order to avoid "giving into my flesh" and inadvertently falling in love with someone, I made a concerted effort to stay away from all female-kind my own age. I had never dated a girl and I never would. Had I imagined what God was up to that night, there is a strong possibility that I may have tried to sabotage His plans. It's a good thing I didn't.

Rebekah told me a year later that she had been going through her own struggles that night. She now tells me that she had to work hard to keep her composure. After dropping various objects and nearly tripping over, she began to wonder what on earth was going on. When her heart refused to stop pounding, she made up her mind to keep her head down and, at all costs, avoid any eye contact.

Well, if it was love at first sight for Rebekah, it was love at third or fourth sight for me. You see, I was a little slow then. I received a friend request from her on messenger after I returned to the States and we chatted from time to time. Although, I barely gave her the time of day she tells me! Rebekah eventually gave up trying to form a friendship and decided to forget about me, believing that she would probably never see me again anyway. Ironically, God began to work in my heart around the same time, and I came to the realization one day that I *didn't* want to be alone for the rest of my life. The opportunity arose to visit Perth again much sooner than I ever expected, and in just a few months I was packing my bags, heading down once more to "The Great South Land of the Holy Spirit."

Then, something odd happened. I was in Perth for the weekend, and during that time I never saw Rebekah, not once. The most unusual thing is that I *noticed.* To my surprise, I even felt a little disappointed when I scanned the crowds and realized she wasn't there. I thought little else about it though, until the third time I returned to Perth. I was staying with my Aussie buddy Justin, who attended Pastor Francisco's church, and was waiting for him to return to the house to pick me up. I looked at the clock nervously – it was starting to get late. Suddenly I heard Justin's car pull into the driveway and I walked outside, ready to leave.

As I approached the car, I noticed someone else sitting next to him in the passenger seat, smiling at me. It was Rebekah! She got out of the car and I surprised myself by giving her a hug. I was even more surprised that it felt like embracing an old friend. I somehow felt very comfortable around her, like I had known her for years. Over the next two days, Rebekah accompanied us to all the meetings and, as she was a young woman who had an obvious thirst for the things of God, I thought little else of it! I was pleased though, as it gave me the opportunity to spend time getting to know her. I was surprised to learn that while attending Francisco's church she had picked up Spanish, quite unusual and admirable for a young Australian woman, I thought. Very quickly, I found that I was forming a high opinion of Rebekah. I would probably never have realized this though, were it not pointed out to me. One evening, after Justin and I dropped Rebekah home from a meeting, Justin turned to me, and, with a sly smile, had the audacity to ask, "You like her, don't you?" As it turned out, Justin had been watching Rebekah and me interact with keen interest and had already come to his own conclusion. "Well I…she's a great person…but…sort of. *Maybe*." The "maybe" was enough for Justin, and I was teased mercilessly all the way home.

After spending a few more days around Rebekah, however, I became convinced that my "maybe" was in fact a "yes."

The trip drew to a close, and the last meeting was over. I would be leaving early the next morning and catching the first flight back to the States. People milled around, enjoying coffee and fellowship and I kept an eye out for Rebekah. She had been there in the meeting, but where was she now? When it came time for us to go home and I still hadn't seen her, I felt very sad.

"Why didn't she even say goodbye?" I wondered. "Maybe she forgot? Or maybe she didn't even care…"

Many years later, Rebekah revealed to me that she *hadn't* forgotten to say goodbye. Instead, convinced this would definitely be the last time she would ever see me, she quietly slipped out the back door of the church and left with her grandmother. Far from caring, she sat in the back seat of the car that night and gazed out into the darkness, the raindrops rolling down the window mirroring her own tears.

Two days later, Rebekah heard the phone ring. Her brother entered the room and passed her the phone, saying, "It's for you."

"Hello."

"Hi, uh, this is Alejandro."

"Alejandro?" she sounded surprised.

"Yes. How are you?"

"I'm good thanks, where are you?"

"I'm in Surabaya, Indonesia right now."

"Wow, that's awesome."

Silence.

"Listen, um, I was wondering if I could ask you a favor."

"Yes?"

"Well, I need to contact your pastor and I have lost his number. Can you give it to me?

"Oh, sure." (Did she sound disappointed?)

"Thanks."

Amazingly, after Rebekah gave me the number, we spoke

for about forty-five minutes. Without me having been able to think of a decent excuse to keep in touch, we said our goodbyes, and reluctantly hung up.

Two days later, I called to ask for the number again, and then the day after that. On the fourth call, I knew I could no longer keep up the façade (Rebekah was by then wondering how I had gotten hold of *her* number!) and I found the courage to tell her that I would like to stay in touch. From that day on, we began to talk regularly on Skype. Over the course of three months, our conversations grew progressively longer. It was beautiful. We prayed for each other, we shared the deepest dreams and aspirations of our hearts and we spoke about our callings. I was delighted to discover that Rebekah and my callings were virtually aligned. Even the time differences didn't deter us; sometimes we spoke until one, two a.m. in the morning. After hanging up reluctantly one evening after a four hour conversation, (praise God that Skype is free!) I realized that I was definitely falling for this pretty Irish/Aussie with the green eyes and black hair. I wanted more than just a friendship with Rebekah. I wanted her to be my wife.

Sounding more like a sixth grader than a twenty-year-old, I shyly asked her if she would be my girlfriend. She agreed enthusiastically, and so we officially began a long distance courtship. Then it became tough – very tough. When the initial euphoria wore off, we realized that we were faced with numerous obstacles. First, we lived on opposite sides of the world. Second, as my travel increased we were often unable to contact each other, sometimes for days or even a week at a time. Third, there were some individuals who strongly opposed our relationship. They were well meaning, but were afraid that one of us or both would get hurt.

On a couple of occasions, we were so discouraged that we considered calling off the relationship. There was one thing that kept us going though – the conviction that we were part of each other's destiny. God confirmed this to Rebekah during a particularly difficult time. She was feeling confused and drained, so she decided to fast and pray for as long as it took to get a clear answer. During that time, she had a vivid dream. In the dream, she saw me placing not one, but three rings on her wedding finger. This gave her the strength to believe that God was absolutely in our relationship, and she fought on.

A Long Wait is Rewarded

Three years and many trans-pacific flights later, we were finally married in a beautiful ceremony in Perth. Surrounded by our friends and family, we worshipped God with all our hearts that day, thanking Him for how far He had brought us. We felt His presence and sensed His blessing over us. One detail stood out for me. We were married in Bethany Church, one of the very first places I had preached at in Perth. God had brought me full circle in my Australian journey, and now my bride and I were about to set out together, reaching the nations for Him.

The Great South Land of the Holy Spirit

Jesus said that we would take the Gospel to ends of the earth. While this verse can be interpreted in a number of ways,

I am certain He was talking about Australia. I hadn't planned to relocate to the world's largest island nation, but it was certainly on God's agenda. Long before I met Rebekah or even visited there, God spoke to me about Australia. Around the time of the Lakeland Revival in Florida, I attended one of the meetings, which ran for a hundred consecutive nights.

That particular night, God gave me a vision. I saw a map of Australia being unrolled before me. After contemplating it for a moment, I saw that each of the four corners was being held by an angel in one hand. With their other hands, they held jars. Each of the four jars held an element, which the angel then began to pour on the map. One poured water, one wine, one oil and the other poured wheat. When all four had cast their elements down, the map caught fire! When I looked into the flames, I saw that they contained what looked like small screens. Each one flashed the picture of a different scene, and I saw whole venues packed with people worshipping Jesus. The images appeared to be revival events taking place all over Australia. After the vision ended, I heard the voice of God, calling me to move to Australia. Undoubtedly, He had spoken, but it would be many confirmations later before I would find the courage to take such a big step. There was one big obstacle holding me back at the time – my own plans. I had it all arranged in my head; I would stay in Dallas, Texas where I was living at the time, (yes, God fulfilled his promise!) and there I would remain firmly rooted. All my plans looked secure; right up until the day God came along and broke up the pieces of my neatly put together jigsaw. I was going to have to start again. God was moving me out of my comfort zone and challenging my faith by asking me to move into the unknown.

After going to Australia for the third time, I was seriously beginning to consider moving there, but it didn't happen until Rebekah and I were married. I wrestled with the idea for two years, but at the end decided it was best to obey God. It is always best to obey God, because blessings will always follow obedience. I was very *comfortable* doing ministry in America, but when God calls you to a new place your comfort has nothing to do with it. The question should not then be *why* you are going there, but *how* you are going to make it there. When God commissions you, there should only be one option, and that is to *GO*.

Chapter 27

Don't Let Your Lamp Go Out

As I continue to travel the world and preach the Gospel today, I have seen a disturbing trend. The lamps of many are going out. We live in an age when many Christians are walking in religion not relationship or going to church to fulfill their emotional needs. Still others spend their time chasing experiences instead of the heart of God or simply wish to receive recognition. Nonetheless, being a Christian is about more than being affiliated with a mega church or just being a regular churchgoer on Sundays. It is about being God's intimate friend. Many do not know how to cultivate a deep relationship with the Lord, simply because they are not taught how to. The Word has become scarce in many churches and the Gospel has been watered down so as not to offend anyone.

We live in a time when God's heart cries out desperately for a generation of "Abrahams" – friends of God who know His voice and catch the vision He longs to bring into being. God has called us all to be visionaries. We must be like the eagles, always seeing with crystal clear vision. We must adopt heaven's perspective, seeing each situation in life from above. In times when the vision is scarce, we need to see with prophetic eyes, looking further than the constraints of the post-modern church and evangelical fashions. Sadly, many Christians have become distracted by these and have abandoned the principle essence and foundations of Christianity.

A True Relationship with Jesus

In the days of the apostles, followers of Jesus Christ became known as Christians, literally "to be a follower of Jesus Christ." There is, however, another important aspect of being a Christian. To bear the name of Christ is to be associated with Him. If we are associated with Jesus, we should be recognized by doing the same things that He did. The first Christians received that name because they walked like Him, talked like Him, prayed like Him, performed signs like Him, acted like Him and lived like Him. In short, they were easily identifiable. *Everything they did testified to their relationship with Jesus and the time they had spent in His presence.*

> "When they saw the courage of Peter and John and realized that they were unschooled, ordinary men, they were astonished and they took note that these men had been with Jesus." Acts 4:13 (NIV)

How glorious it would be, if the church today returned to

the ways of the primitive church, just as it was in the days of the apostles! The wonderful news is, it will. Even as the love of many grows cold (Matthew 24:12) God will rise up a core remnant who will return to the signs and wonders of the first church. The darker the world becomes around us, the brighter the light of Jesus Christ will shine. Just as prophesied by the prophet Habakkuk, God is bringing a great awakening to the whole world and "the earth will be filled with the knowledge of the glory of the Lord, as the waters cover the sea." Habakkuk 2:14 (NIV)

Beloved, we are now in one of the most glorious seasons on earth, "the season of reaping." The Gospel *has* been and *is* being sown throughout the world and we are invited to take part in the harvest. As we work and wait, we are to prepare for the coming of our beloved Savior, Jesus Christ. We must ensure that we are ready, washing our robes with the redeeming blood of Jesus every day.

Today, more than ever, God seeks "worshippers in spirit and in truth." (John 4:24) Anything which must be sought out is not readily visible or available. This would imply that true worshippers are sometimes hard for God to find. How strange this is, when the temple veil has been torn, the door opened, and every human being can freely approach God's throne by His grace and mercy!

God seeks a people with a determined, active and enduring faith to entrust with the riches of His Kingdom. It is time for you to take hold of the inheritance God has promised you! In order to do it, you must be prepared to grow spiritually and use your faith aggressively to claim the victory that has already been won for you.

> "With God we will gain the victory, and he will trample down our enemies." Psalm 60:12 (NIV).

In order to have a robust faith, one ready to be activated at all times, we must fortify it with the Word. As Romans 10:17 says, "Faith comes from hearing the message." We must also strengthen our faith by using it. Faith is like a muscle that needs to be exercised in order to be strong and avoid deteriorating.

If God has given you a plan, this is the time for you to accomplish it, arising in Jesus' name and making a difference in your community. Take hold of the dreams God has given you and run with them! Do not limit His power at work in your life, for the Lord longs to use you to reach the world with His salvation. Let us work together in the spirit of cooperation, laboring to the end of winning the nations for Christ, the King of Kings and Lord of Lords.

Healing and Revival meetings in Cali, Colombia.

Preaching on faith in Sydney, Australia.

Healing crusade at Bethany Church, Surabaya, Indonesia.

Revival meetings at Resurrection and Life Church, Curaçao.

Healing Crusade in Quito, Ecuador, at His Presence Church.

A man deaf in his right ear is healed miraculously. Harare, Zimbabwe.

Preaching at Living Water Ministries in Rotterdam, Netherlands.

Rebekah and me with our daughter, Carielle Arias.

About Author

Alejandro Arias was born in San Jose, Costa Rica in 1987. At the age of seven he gave his heart to the Lord, following his mother's conversion. Just months later their faith would be severely tested, when it was discovered that Alejandro had a cancerous tumor lodged between his heart and lungs. Convinced that God had a destiny for his life in spite of the circumstances, he began to pray each day, believing God for his healing. When Alejandro was re-examined three months later, the doctors found that the tumor had miraculously disappeared.

Following his supernatural encounter with the power of God, Alejandro received the baptism of the Holy Spirit and began to develop a passion for passing out tracts and sharing the gospel. A Venezuelan missionary called Orlando Lopez saw the call of God on the young boy's life and began to mentor him, giving him opportunities to preach to hundreds at evangelistic outreaches in a local park. In 1999, Orlando felt led to take Alejandro with him to Venezuela to preach at evangelistic crusades. Many salvations and healings resulted.

Alejandro then began to preach and travel all over his native Costa Rica, covering almost the entire country with the gospel over the course of two years. At this time he also began to visit surrounding Latin American countries, such as Nicaragua, Guatemala and Colombia.

In 2002, Alejandro sensed the Lord calling him to make the United States home. AAIM continued to expand after the move, with opportunities arising to minister in countries such as Zimbabwe, Indonesia, Spain, Chile, Finland and Italy and others.

While in Lakeland, Florida in 2007, Alejandro saw a vision of the map of Australia and was prompted to travel to the island nation for the first time. This would be the first of many trips, one of which would see the Lord introducing him to his future wife, Rebekah.

In 2011 Alejandro and Rebekah were married in Perth, Australia among their friends and family. They travelled and ministered internationally for six months before returning to Australia to settle in Melbourne, Victoria.

Alejandro and Rebekah are blessed to see the doors that God is opening in Melbourne, all over Australia and in previously unvisited nations. This is an exciting season and they can't wait to see what God has in store for the future! Alejandro and Rebekah are the proud parents of a beautiful baby girl named Carielle Lee Arias.

They attend South West Christian Church in Werribee with Pastors Malcolm and Karen Mcloud. Alejandro is currently a credentialed minister with the Assemblies of God in Australia, better known as the Australian Christian Churches.

For more information about Alejandro Arias:
AAIM Ministries USA
P. O. Box 120660
Clermont, FL 34712-0660
Phone: (214) 296-4019
Website: www.alejandroarias.net

AAIM Ministries Australia
64 Regal Road
Point Cook Vic, 3030

Phone: (61) 490-133-453

Website: www.alejandroarias.net

Need additional copies?

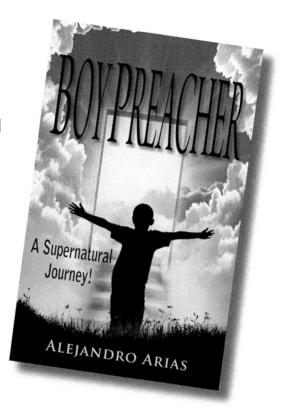

To order more copies of

BOY PREACHER,

contact NewBookPublishing.com

❏ Order online at
NewBookPublishing.com/Bookstore

❏ Call 877-311-5100 or

❏ Email Info@NewBookPublishing.com